# ADVANCED SWIMMING

## Steps to Success

David G. Thomas, MS
Professor Emeritus
State University of New York–Binghamton

**Leisure Press**
Champaign, Illinois

**Library of Congress Cataloging-in-Publication Data**

Thomas, David G., 1924-
    Advanced swimming : steps to success / by David G. Thomas.
      p.  cm.
    Follows: Swimming. c1989.
    ISBN 0-88011-389-8
    1. Swimming--Study and teaching.  I. Thomas, David G., 1924-
Swimming.  II. Title.
    GV836.35.T46  1990
    797.2'1--dc20                              90-31279
                                               CIP

ISBN: 0-88011-389-8

**Developmental Editor:** Judy Patterson Wright, PhD; **Copyeditor:** Peter Nelson; **Assistant Editors:** Julia Anderson, Valerie Hall, and Robert King; **Proofreader:** Laurie McGee; **Production Director:** Ernie Noa; **Typesetter:** Sandra Meier; **Text Design:** Keith Blomberg; **Text Layout:** Tara Welsch; **Cover Design:** Jack Davis; **Cover Model:** Carol Bossert; **Cover Photo:** Wilmer Zehr; **Illustrations:** Tim Offenstein; **Printer:** United Graphics

Instructional Designer for the Steps to Success Activity Series: Joan N. Vickers, EdD, University of Calgary, Calgary, Alberta, Canada

Printed in the United States of America    10  9  8  7  6

**Leisure Press**
**A Division of Human Kinetics**
Web site: http://www.humankinetics.com/

*United States:* Human Kinetics, P.O. Box 5076, Champaign, IL 61825-5076
1-800-747-4457
e-mail: humank@hkusa.com

*Canada:* Human Kinetics, Box 24040, Windsor, ON N8Y 4Y9
1-800-465-7301 (in Canada only)
e-mail: humank@hkcanada.com

*Europe:* Human Kinetics, P.O. Box IW14, Leeds LS16 6TR, United Kingdom
(44) 1132 781708
e-mail: humank@hkeurope.com

*Australia:* Human Kinetics, 57A Price Avenue, Lower Mitcham, South Australia 5062
(08) 277 1555
e-mail: humank@hkaustralia.com

*New Zealand:* Human Kinetics, P.O. Box 105-231, Auckland 1
(09) 523 3462
e-mail: humank@hknewz.com

# Contents

# Preface

This is a second-level swimming text. It follows the highly successful *Swimming: Steps to Success*. That text guided the beginning swimmer on a step-by-step process for learning the basic fundamentals of swimming and introduced the elementary backstroke, the crawl, the sidestroke, and the breaststroke.

*Advanced Swimming: Steps to Success* contains a step-by-step process for learning new competitive strokes (back and butterfly), reviewing the crawl and the breaststroke and improving them to competitive levels, and learning the competitive turns. In addition, for those who want to be master swimming technicians, this book follows the evolutionary order in which swimming strokes were developed: It teaches or reviews the breaststroke, the sidestroke, the less commonly known overhand sidestroke, and the series of trudgen strokes.

This book also opens the door to a non-traditional world of watermanship that may intrigue and fascinate the creative participant. Watermanship, the mastery of the aquatic element, will produce profound changes in the philosophy and lifestyle of anyone who studies it.

In *Swimming* (1904, p. 64), Ralph Thomas quoted the following from William Wilson's 1883 book, *The Swimming Instructor*: ''The experienced swimmer, when in the water, may be classed among the happiest of mortals in the happiest of moods, and in the most complete enjoyment of the happiest of exercises.'' Continue the happy experience now with *Advanced Swimming: Steps to Success*.

On completion of this series of steps, you will be ready to participate in the other facets of the wonderful world of water: lifesaving, lifeguarding, speed swimming, synchronized swimming, scuba diving, swimming for the disabled, and water activities such as water polo, underwater hockey, and water skiing.

I must acknowledge the contributions of those who helped in producing this book. Dr. Judy Patterson Wright, my developmental editor, kept me headed in the right direction. The copyeditor corrected and rearranged my grammar and phrasing, and the other staff members at Leisure Press put the book together and made it look inviting. I must also thank Steve Wycoff, Stuart Fowler, and Jana McKinney—the staff at the Sheppard Swim Center in Anderson, South Carolina—for their help in developing some of the drills.

This book is dedicated to Becky and David and others of their generation who will find the joy, the freedom, and the healthy glow that aquatics and true watermanship bring to life.

# The Steps to Success Staircase

You have climbed the swimming staircase to the first landing. Now prepare to continue your journey to excellence. This text will lead you into the highest level of competitive swimming strokes and turns. It will also lead you from exacting, high-tech strokes into the fun-filled realm of aquatic tricks and stunts.

Read carefully the sections entitled "Watermanship," "Safety Considerations and Equipment," and "Preparing Your Body for Success" before you begin. Then, when you understand the concept of watermanship, are cognizant of the safety rules, and know how to prepare your body for learning, begin with Step 1. Remain at each step until you have achieved all of its drill Success Goals, then move easily up to the next challenge in the following step.

Follow the same sequence each step of the way:

1. Read the explanation of why that step is important.
2. Follow the numbered illustrations that break down exactly how to position and move your body to perform each basic skill successfully. There are three phases or parts to each breakdown: preparation (getting into position), execution (performing the skill), and follow-through (recovery).
3. Practice the drills specifically designed to help you achieve success at each step. They help you improve your skills through repetition.
4. Record your drill scores after you practice each drill. Compare your score with the Success Goal for the drill.
5. After mastering each skill, ask an expert, such as your teacher or coach, to evaluate your skill technique qualitatively according to the Keys to Success Checklists. Then your evaluator may tailor specific goals for you.
6. Continue this process through all the steps in this book. Once you have completed all the steps, rate yourself, then ask your evaluator to rate your combined skill execution according to the "Rating Your Total Progress" directions.

Good luck on your step-by-step journey to increasing your swimming skills, success, confidence, and fun. Climb at your own pace and enjoy each step along the way.

# Watermanship: A Departure From Traditional Aquatics Courses

"Let's go swimming," I called.

"O.K., Dad."

My son picked up his trunks, towel, and goggles and beat me to the car. He's quite a swimmer, you know. Took first place in the country club championships this summer. Swims the medley. Knows all the strokes.

As we stepped onto the pool deck, his friends greeted him with all the respect due his newly won position.

"Hi, Ed. How ya doin'?"

"Hey, there's the champ. C'mon in. Water's great."

Ed proceeded to stretch his shoulders, shake out his hands and arms, windmill a few times; shake one leg and foot, then the other; and strut up to the shallow end of the pool. After three deep breaths, he assumed the start position, paused long enough to be sure everyone was watching, and did a smooth racing dive into the pool. He swam the butterfly to the other end, came back in backstroke, switched to breaststroke for the third length, and brought it home in "freestyle" crawl. Having completed his individual medley, Ed was finished. That's what swimming is; he had been swimming. Now it was time to sit in the sun and turn brown.

If you were to ask Ed to show you some other strokes or to demonstrate a feetfirst torpedo scull, you might get to see the sidestroke he learned for lifesaving class, but the mention of sculling, rolling, somersaulting, or any other of the hundreds of fun skills would bring forth only a blank stare. Yet, he is the champ. He is the "swimming expert" that others look upon as a model.

Watermanship, the ability to be at home in—to become one with—the water, is the most rewarding of the aquatic arts. The ability to float, twist, bend, roll, sink, rise, and spin in weightless suspension can bring immense joy and relaxation to a troubled or fatigued body. There are times when my students tell me they think I have hidden gills when I demonstrate a new skill I discovered that morning. There are times when I feel almost ready to believe them when I contemplate the part watermanship has played in my life. I can easily be led to believe that people have evolved from denizens of the deep and that my love for the water is a symbolic "return to the womb."

Watermanship includes exploration, experimentation, and evolution of strokes, stunts, tricks, and motions, and ultimate enjoyment of aquatic pursuits. It is of inestimable value to aquatics students to allow them to analyze stroke movements and to perform in ultraslow motion the exact movements and sequences involved in any stroke. Once this ability is mastered, learning any new stroke becomes a very simple matter indeed.

To encourage a sense of watermanship in my students, I frequently assign them a "trick of the day" to master before the next lesson—on their own time. Sometimes they have more fun and spend more time in mastering the trick of the day than on their more formal class assignment. You can devise hundreds of simple problems, challenges, and stunts that require and exhibit mastery of the aquatic environment—watermanship.

Many, such as Ed, have never learned to have fun in the water. They have learned how to swim to consummate boredom through 10,000 yards a day in search of a medal, but they have never learned to relax, to enjoy, revel in, lose one's self in the softest, kindest, friendliest, of nature's gifts to humankind—clear, pure, temperate water.*

This text addresses skills and progressions leading to proficiency in the strokes displayed by Ed in the preceding story, but it is also designed to do much more than that. In addition to the standard, ''packaged'' traditional strokes, this text will lead you on an adventure in watermanship. You will be introduced to skills that transcend the traditional and awaken you to a new joy in accomplishment. Understanding and participating in creative activity in the aquatic medium comes about as close to developing a ''philosophy of swimming'' as anything I know.

Perhaps the greatest example of the watermanship concept among the water sports of today is synchronized swimming, which continually evolves through exploration of new motions and positions in the water. Here, perhaps more than in any other phase of aquatics, watermanship is a factor in performance. This text will introduce you to a few of the elementary stunts found in synchronized swimming, starting with the basic movements of universal sculling.

David G. Thomas

---

*This article is adapted and reprinted with permission from the *Journal of Physical Education, Recreation & Dance*, May 1980, page 63. The *Journal* is a publication of the American Alliance for Health, Physical Education, Recreation and Dance, 1900 Association Drive, Reston, VA 22091.

# Safety Considerations and Equipment

Safety rules can be vital to your health, and items of equipment that may be helpful or essential to your learning progress should be mentioned early. Here are helpful words on those subjects.

## SAFETY

It is generally acknowledged that good swimmers are safer than nonswimmers, but being a good swimmer does not guarantee immunity from drowning. Even the best of swimmers can find themselves in situations caused by injury or fatigue that can lead to distress and drowning. Fear of water is not useful, but a healthy respect for its consistent, relentless following of physical laws is advisable. Caution is the key to safety. The following precautionary rules are axiomatic in aquatics for showing proper respect for the medium:

- Never swim alone. Always have with you someone who can help, or can get help, in an emergency.
- Know the area where you plan to swim. Know where the deep and shallow areas are, and find out about any hidden hazards that are not apparent from above the water. Learn about currents, eddies, tides, and runouts that are peculiar to the area.
- Never chew gum while swimming. Breathing patterns in swimming require a clear mouth and throat.
- Never overestimate your ability or endurance. Don't assume that your endurance is the same at the beginning of a swim season as it was at the end of the last season. Start easy.
- Never swim immediately after a heavy meal. Wait at least 30 minutes after a light meal and longer after a heavy meal.
- Use great care in diving and do not dive into water less than 5 feet deep.

- Do not run, push, or indulge in horseplay on a pool deck. The area is usually wet and slippery, and accidents can easily happen.

## EQUIPMENT

The following items of equipment will be used in *Advanced Swimming: Steps to Success*:

- Kickboard
- Float belt
- Leg float
- Face mask
- Snorkel
- Goggles
- Nose clip
- Swim fins and socks or boots
- Stopwatch or timer
- Stretch cord or surgical tubing

If you have been using the text *Swimming: Steps to Success* as a guide to learning how to swim, you are already familiar with many of these items. Kickboards, leg floats, timers, and goggles are standard items for competitive swim training. Swim masks, swim fins, and snorkels are standard skin diving and scuba diving items. Nose clips are used by all synchronized swimmers. You will use a piece of stretch cord or surgical tubing about 10 feet long in learning the back crawl armstroke; it is helpful but not essential. We will use the pictured items as learning aids (see Figure 1).

Masks, fins, and boots are the only expensive items on the list. They are personal-fit items and must be fitted to your needs by a knowledgeable professional. Snorkels, goggles, and nose clips are also personal items from the standpoint of fit and hygiene, but they are relatively inexpensive. Kickboards and leg floats are universal-fit items and can most likely be borrowed from the pool operator.

They are also inexpensive, however, and it would be useful to have your own. A stopwatch or timer will be used several times, but you can probably borrow one. Many wristwatches have built-in timers.

**Figure 1** Learning aids clockwise from left: Socks to wear with fins, swim fins, face mask and snorkel, leg float, float belt, surgical stretch cords, kickboard, goggles, nose clip, stopwatch (or timer), and a pair of boots to wear with fins.

# Preparing Your Body for Success

Drills for each step in this text will be somewhat more difficult than the drills listed in the beginner text. In addition to the improvement in technique you will achieve, you will benefit from increased body conditioning, flexibility, and endurance and a general sense of well-being. To receive these benefits, you need to prepare your body for the activity and to taper the end of your work period to stretch and relax the muscles involved. A 10- to 15-minute warm-up period before each day's learning period, and a 5-minute taper afterward, should be sufficient.

## WARMING UP

Your warm-up period should consist of breathing exercises to increase your breath control and lung capacity, flexibility exercises to enhance the flexibility of your joints, and strength-building exercises to increase the blood flow in your muscles and make them ready for activity. Do one or two of the following breathing exercises, one or two flexibility exercises for each body part named, and one or two strength exercises for each body part. Use a different series of exercises on each day. Thus, your total warm-up will consist of about six or eight exercises done for 1 or 2 minutes each.

### Breathing Exercises

1. Stand erect, arms at your sides. As you take a deep breath, lift both arms slowly outward and upward until they meet directly overhead. Bring your arms back down in the same path as you exhale slowly. Repeat 10 times, trying to inhale more deeply with each breath.

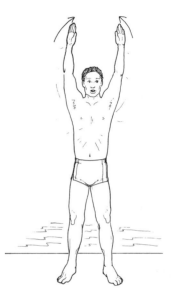

2. Stand erect, hands on your hips and feet spread about 24 inches. Exhale slowly as you bend forward from your hips until your upper torso is horizontal. Inhale deeply as you return slowly to an erect position. Repeat 10 times, trying to inhale more deeply each time.

3. Stand erect, hands clasped behind your head. Take a deep breath and hold it while you count 5 seconds. Exhale very quickly and completely, then inhale fully as quickly as you can. Repeat 10 times, holding each breath for 5 seconds. Emphasize the quickness with which you get rid of one breath and get the next.

### Flexibility Exercises

The two areas in which flexibility is especially required for swimming are the shoulders and the ankles. The following exercises will aid in developing such flexibility.

### Shoulders

1. Stand facing a wall, your stomach tight against the wall and one arm extended straight out at shoulder height, the palm flat against the wall (a). Keep the front of your extended arm tight against the wall as you turn your body away from the arm (b). Continue to turn until you feel firm resistance at the shoulder. Hold the pressure for 5 seconds and release. Repeat 3 times, then do the same exercise with your other arm.

a

b

2. Hold your towel by opposite corners in front of you. Maintain your hold as you raise the towel over your head and bring it down behind you. Then bring it back over your head to the front again. Repeat 4 times. If your shoulders are very supple, shorten your grip on the towel until you feel tension in the shoulders. If your shoulders are very tight, bend an elbow as needed to get the towel behind you.

### Ankles

1. Roll up a towel and place it underneath a chair or open bench. Sit on the chair or bench with your ankles extended and your toes resting on the rolled towel. Relax your ankles and press gently downward on your toes to slightly stretch the front of the ankle joint. Hold the pressure for 30 seconds, then relax. Repeat 3 times.
2. From a prone (facedown) position with your ankles extended and the tops of your toes resting on a folded towel, press up into an extended push-up position. Do not let your hips sag. Hold the

push-up position for 10 seconds, then rest. Be aware of the stretching sensation on the front of your ankles. Repeat 4 times.

3. Stand facing a wall, at arm's length from it. Place a rolled towel under the balls of your feet. Put both hands against the wall and slowly lean into the wall without allowing your heels to leave the deck. Continue to lean toward the wall until you feel firm stretching in the muscles at the back of your legs. Hold stretch for 10 seconds, then push slightly away. Repeat lean 5 times. If you don't feel any stretch, move farther from the wall.

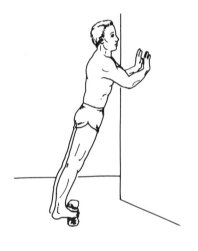

## Strength Exercises

Strength exercises should be done *after* the breathing and flexibility exercises. When strengthening muscles for swimming, you must use care to work on the specific muscles that control motions used in swimming. A swim bench designed specifically for providing resistance while you simulate swimming motions is the most efficient strength builder for swimmers. Pulley weights and stretch cords, however, are ideal for the task, more economical, and can be more easily obtained or made (see Figures 2a-e). You may do the following exercises on the swim bench, with pulley weights, or with stretch cords.

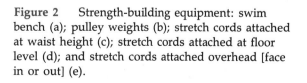

**a**

**b**

**c**

**d**                                    (Cont.)

**Figure 2**    Strength-building equipment: swim bench (a); pulley weights (b); stretch cords attached at waist height (c); stretch cords attached at floor level (d); and stretch cords attached overhead [face in or out] (e).

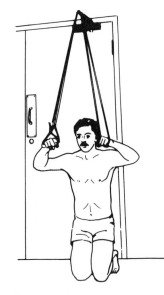

**e**

Figure 2 (Continued)

1. Your body position during this exercise depends upon the point of attachment of the stretch cords or pulley weights, which may be at waist height, at floor level, or overhead. In any case, start with both arms extended fully overhead. Pull both arms simultaneously through the exact path for the underwater portion of a correct crawl armstroke. If you are using short stretch cords, you may have to pull only through the top half of the armstroke for 10 pulls, then move closer to the attachment point to do the bottom half of the pull. Use enough weight, or move far enough from the attachment point of the stretch cords, so that 10 pulls is about all you can do. If the 10th pull is easy, add more weight or stretch the cords more. Pull slowly, and force your arms to return slowly with the pull of the weights or cords. Perform the 10-pull sequence twice, with a 30-second rest.

2. Stand erect with the pulley or cord attachment directly overhead. Start with your arms stretched fully overhead. Pull out to the sides and down to your thighs in a pull similar to that of the elementary backstroke. As soon as you start pulling, bend your elbows somewhat but do not allow your hands to come in front of your body. Keep your elbows high so you are pushing rather than pulling against the resistance. Do not allow your elbows to move ahead of your hands at any point.

3. Using the same apparatus as for the two previous exercises, simulate the pull for the breaststroke. You may use the stretch cords from either a standing or a lying position. Do two sets of 10 pulls, with a 30-second rest between sets.

## TAPERING

A short taper, or cool-down, period should follow each lesson or practice session. Some suggestions follow:

1. Just before leaving the pool, swim 2 lengths trying to see how slowly you can go, with a long, restful glide between strokes.
2. Bob and breathe slowly for 30 breaths.
3. Lie back and float motionless, completely relaxed, for 30 seconds.

*Step 1* # Improving the Crawl Stroke

Since this book is a second-level text, some knowledge of a rudimentary crawl stroke is assumed. Familiarity with a flutter kick, an overhand armstroke, and crawl stroke breathing will be helpful, but all these items are reviewed here. If you used the basic-level text, *Swimming: Steps to Success*, you learned all of the preliminary skills. Now it is time to improve and polish the stroke to an advanced level.

## WHY IS A SMOOTH CRAWL STROKE IMPORTANT?

The crawl stroke is the epitome, the very image, of swimming. It is the fastest stroke known and the stroke by which your swimming prowess will be judged. The average person on the pool deck will not be impressed with the strength of your scissors kick or the length of your breaststroke glide, but will notice immediately how smoothly and easily you swim the crawl.

## HOW TO SWIM THE CRAWL STROKE EFFICIENTLY

To swim well, you must remember that you are not swimming to stay up but that your buoyancy will keep you at the surface whether you swim or not. Therefore, you begin the crawl stroke with an easy, relaxed prone glide. We will next examine in sequence the correct patterns for kicking, stroking, arm-leg coordination, and breathing.

### Kicking

Begin kicking rhythmically with an easy, relaxed crawl stroke kick. Keep your ankles perfectly relaxed so each foot flops from the ankle. Let your knee bend slightly on the downward phase of the kick. The water pressure from the downward movement will press against the instep of your foot and force the toes into an extended position. Your knee should stop its downward movement at a depth of approximately 9 inches, and the lower leg, ankle, and foot should continue downward until the knee is straight.

At the exact moment that the knee straightens, the entire straight leg begins its upward thrust. As the leg begins to move upward, your ankle, still perfectly relaxed, bends as the pressure of the water pushes on the sole of your foot. Your leg should continue to move upward until the heel is at the surface. As your heel reaches the surface, upward motion ceases and a new kick begins. The other leg follows the same pattern exactly but works in opposition.

### Stroking

The armstroke may begin with either arm. For the sake of clarity and brevity, though, we will describe the stroke as beginning with the right arm and moving through an S-shaped path (see Figure 1.1).

Begin stroking from a prone glide position with both arms extended overhead, hands about 6 inches under the surface. Allow the hands to be relaxed, but with fingers straight.

Figure 1.1 S-shaped arm path.

Do not squeeze the fingers tightly together; a small space between them will not affect the pulling power but will allow greater relaxation.

Bend your right wrist and rotate the entire arm medially (inward), pointing your fingers downward and outward at about 45 degrees. As your arm rotates, allow a slight bend in your elbow, which will turn your hand slightly palm out. Lock your wrist, hand, and elbow rigidly in that position and move your arm outward so the hand moves laterally about 10 or 12 inches. This outward motion, if done properly, produces pressure on the palm of the hand; this sculling motion uses Bernoulli's principle (which is also a factor in airplane wing lift) to create a pulling force over the back of your hand. This first propulsive force of the armstroke is shown from two viewpoints in Figures 1.2a and b.

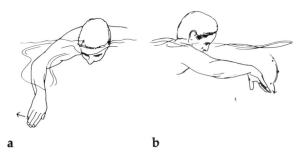

**a**                          **b**

**Figure 1.2**  First propulsive force of the armstroke from the front (a) and the side (b).

As your hand reaches the end of its short outward movement, smoothly rotate the forearm, straighten the wrist, and bend the elbow to an angle of about 100 degrees so your fingertips point downward and slightly inward. Your hand slices downward, across, and backward to the centerline of your body at about the level of your chin. This movement is partially sculling motion and partially pulling motion. The sculling component of the movement adds Bernoulli lift forces to the back of the hand while the palm of the hand is pressing backward. This is a very important part of the propulsive force of the armstroke (see Figures 1.3a and b).

The elbow continues to bend 90 degrees as your entire arm begins to pull from the shoulder. At this point the upper arm should be at the level of the shoulder but slanted slightly

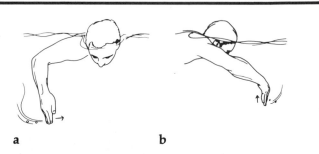

**a**                          **b**

**Figure 1.3**  Second propulsive force of the armstroke from the front (a) and the side (b).

outward so that, with the elbow bent 90 degrees, your hand is directly under your chin, on the centerline of your body. Now your arm is at its best position for pulling force. Your entire arm—forearm, wrist, hand, and upper arm—is perpendicular to the direction of pull (see Figures 1.4a and b). Pull your arm directly backward with the hand about 6 inches under the centerline of your body. At this point the pull transforms into a push.

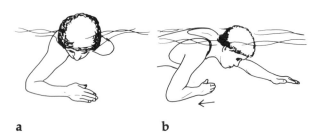

**a**                          **b**

**Figure 1.4**  Front (a) and side (b) views of the propulsive force generated by the entire arm.

As the push progresses, your wrist begins to relax, and water pressure bends your wrist back so the palm remains perpendicular to the direction of push (see Figure 1.5). Your elbow must straighten to continue pushing, and your hand moves outward to a position just beside your upper thigh. During the pull-push, your

**Figure 1.5**  Propulsive force of the hand.

upper body should be rolling so your right shoulder rolls clear of the surface. At this end-of-pull position, your thumb should be within an inch of your thigh, your elbow should be straight, and your palm should be facing upward (see Figure 1.6).

Figure 1.6   End-of-pull position.

Begin the armstroke recovery using only your shoulder muscles and lifting your elbow directly up and forward, allowing the elbow, wrist, and hand to be perfectly relaxed (see Figure 1.7). Be sure to retain full medial (inward) rotation of your arm from the shoulder as your arm moves forward until the forearm is at shoulder level. As your hand passes your shoulder on its way forward, begin to straighten your elbow, keep your right shoulder elevated, and begin to reach ''over the barrel'' to touch the water with your fingertips as far forward of your head as possible (see Figure 1.8). Do not drop your elbow until your fingertips touch the water and you begin your roll to the opposite side. As your right hand enters the water, stretch forward with arm *and* shoulder to reach and hold a straight position about 6 inches deep.

Figure 1.7   Initial armstroke recovery.

Figure 1.8   Over-the-barrel reach position.

Begin to pull with your left arm when the fingertips of your right hand are still about 8 inches above the water on the right-arm recovery. The left armstroke follows an S-shaped pull-push pattern identical to that of the right arm (see Figure 1.1)

### Arm-Leg Coordination

The modern crawl stroke allows more leeway in selecting an arm-leg coordination pattern than when the classic 6-beat American crawl or the older 4-beat Australian crawl were taught. The importance of the crawl stroke kick is diminishing as we realize that it requires more energy than its propulsive force is worth. There is great variance in the coordination patterns used by world-class swimmers. Some, especially sprinters, use the classic 6-beat stroke. Others, especially distance swimmers, use a 4- or 2-beat stroke, and some appear to use the kick only for balance. We will describe the classic 6-beat American crawl stroke, but if the coordination proves too cumbersome to master, it is perfectly acceptable for you to adopt a different kick pattern that is more natural for you.

### American Crawl Stroke Coordination

Until it becomes an habitual pattern, you will have to count each downward leg beat in a 6-count cycle. Begin the pull of your right arm as your left leg kicks downward on the count of 1. Allow your left arm to remain in a relaxed, straight glide position. Pull your right arm through as your right leg kicks downward on the kick count of 2, and recover it as your left leg kicks downward during the 3rd count. Your right hand should reenter the water in front of the shoulder, fingertips first, on the right-leg count of 4. Your left arm begins its pull just prior to the count of 4 from a glide position with the hand about 8 inches deep, pulls through on the left-leg count of 5, recovers on the right-leg count of 6, and reenters the water on the next count of 1. Emphasize 1 and 4 as the key counts in maintaining coordination between arm and leg movements. Note that each arm begins its pull as the other is about to enter the water.

### Breathing

Breathing is coordinated with the armstroke. Turn your head on the count of 1 or 4 and inhale on the count of 2 or 5, depending on whether you wish to breathe on your left or your right side. Note that your head should *turn*, not *lift*, for a breath. Inhalation on the count of 2 (or 5) indicates that you take the breath during the last half of the pull, not during the recovery of the arm. At the count of 2 (or 5), your arm is finishing its power stroke, the hand still in the water, and your shoulders are rolled to facilitate lifting your arm in recovery.

If you were to wait to breathe until your arm was in the air for recovery, the added weight of an arm not supported by buoyancy would necessitate a supporting downward push of the forward hand to keep your mouth above water. Your forward arm would then be too deep when the next pull was started. Consequently, coordination and some propulsive force would be lost.

Roll your head back into the water on the count of 4 (or 1). Exhalation should begin immediately when your face submerges, but there is an option on the style of exhalation. Some swimmers prefer to exhale steadily during the entire pull of the arm on the non-breathing side. Others prefer to allow only a trickle of air to escape during most of the time that this arm is pulling, holding most of the air until just before the face breaks water for the next breath. They then get rid of the major portion of the held air in an explosive, forceful exhalation as the mouth rises through the surface. The latter method of breathing, called the ''explosive'' method, has the advantage of forcefully expelling water from around the mouth, making it less likely that the swimmer will inhale water.

### EMPHASIZING SMOOTHNESS AND EASE OF SWIMMING

For a smooth and relaxed stroke, remember to keep your head on the water with one ear submerged, maintain the shoulder roll position until your fingertips are about to enter the water, raise your elbow high, allow the entire lower arm and hand to be completely relaxed on the recovery, and reach forward over the barrel so your fingertips enter the water before your elbow. Make the forward progress fluid and smooth by pulling horizontally back, and eliminate any bobbing tendency by eliminating all downward force on the water (see Figure 1.9).

*Figure 1.9  Keys to Success:*
*Crawl Stroke*

**Preparation
Phase**

1. Float prone, counting
   kicks ____

## Execution
## Phase
### (breathing on the left side)

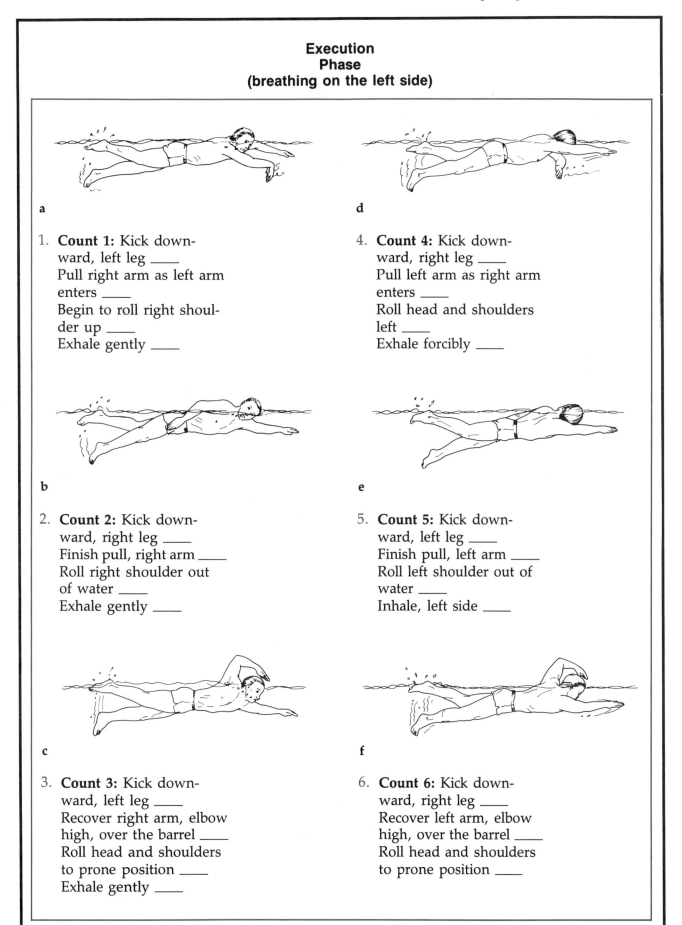

a

1. **Count 1:** Kick downward, left leg ____
   Pull right arm as left arm enters ____
   Begin to roll right shoulder up ____
   Exhale gently ____

b

2. **Count 2:** Kick downward, right leg ____
   Finish pull, right arm ____
   Roll right shoulder out of water ____
   Exhale gently ____

c

3. **Count 3:** Kick downward, left leg ____
   Recover right arm, elbow high, over the barrel ____
   Roll head and shoulders to prone position ____
   Exhale gently ____

d

4. **Count 4:** Kick downward, right leg ____
   Pull left arm as right arm enters ____
   Roll head and shoulders left ____
   Exhale forcibly ____

e

5. **Count 5:** Kick downward, left leg ____
   Finish pull, left arm ____
   Roll left shoulder out of water ____
   Inhale, left side ____

f

6. **Count 6:** Kick downward, right leg ____
   Recover left arm, elbow high, over the barrel ____
   Roll head and shoulders to prone position ____

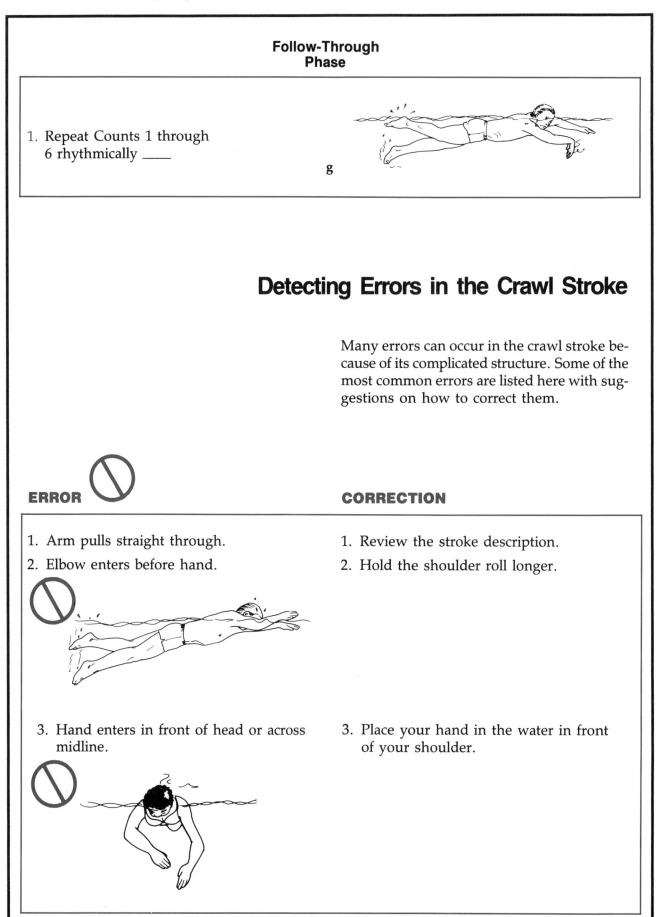

**Follow-Through**
**Phase**

1. Repeat Counts 1 through
   6 rhythmically _____

g

# Detecting Errors in the Crawl Stroke

Many errors can occur in the crawl stroke because of its complicated structure. Some of the most common errors are listed here with suggestions on how to correct them.

**ERROR**

**CORRECTION**

1. Arm pulls straight through.

2. Elbow enters before hand.

1. Review the stroke description.

2. Hold the shoulder roll longer.

3. Hand enters in front of head or across midline.

3. Place your hand in the water in front of your shoulder.

| ERROR | CORRECTION |
|---|---|
| 4. You breathe water. | 4. Breathe during the last half of the pull. |
| 5. Arm recovery is low or wide. | 5. Roll your shoulders more. |
| 6. Arms are "windmilling." | 6. Hold your forward arm in place until just before your recovering arm enters. |
| 7. Arm pull is short. | 7. Pull until your thumb touches your thigh. |

# Crawl Stroke Drills

## 1. Crawl Stroke Kick Drill

Hold a kickboard in front with both hands. Start with a prone glide and kick easily. Use a moderate, 30-degree bend of the knee, bending only on the downward kick. Kick from your hips and allow your ankles to be completely relaxed, feet flopping. Keep your legs close together laterally. Allow your feet to separate vertically about 18 to 20 inches, knees about 9 to 10 inches. Breathe as is convenient.

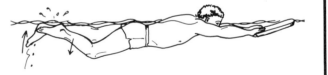

Count "one" as your breathing-side leg kicks downward and continue counting on each downward kick in 6-count sequences. Allow your body to roll slightly; emphasize Counts 1 and 4 greatly at first, then gradually diminish the emphasis. Be sure to count every kick. If you lose count, stop and restart more slowly. Do not be discouraged if you get little propulsion—do not try to kick for speed. Continue to kick easily in a relaxed manner. Turn and push off at each end of the pool.

**Success Goal =**

100 yards or meters of nonstop kicking

**Your Score =**

(#) ____ yards or meters

## 2. *Crawl Kick With Swim Fins and Kickboard*

Don a pair of swim fins (wear athletic socks or scuba boots to prevent chafing). Hold a kickboard in front of you with both arms on top of the board and fingers grasping the front edge. Keep your head up; rest your chin on the trailing edge of the board if you wish. Kick rhythmically with relaxed ankles, counting 6-count cycles. Try to inhale for 2 counts and exhale for 4. Do not allow much knee bend, and try to keep your fins underwater. Kick slowly and easily.

**Success Goal** = 200 yards or meters of nonstop kicking

**Your Score** = (#) _____ yards or meters

## 3. *Crawl Kick With Mask, Fins, and Snorkel*

Don socks or boots, fins, a defogged mask, and a snorkel. Allow your hands to trail alongside your thighs or clasp them behind your back as you kick in 6-count cycles. Keep your chin up slightly as you look ahead and slightly down. Inhale for 2 counts and exhale for 4. Use your hands at the end of each pool length to help you turn and push off.

**Success Goal** =

200 yards or meters of nonstop kicking

**Your Score** =

(#) _____ yards or meters

## 4. *Crawl Kick and Stroke With Non-Breathing-Side Arm, Using Mask, Snorkel, and Kickboard*

Don a defogged mask and a snorkel. Hold a kickboard at arm's length with both hands. Kick rhythmically in 6-count cycles beginning with your *breathing-side leg*. After two full kick cycles, pull with your *non-breathing-side arm* on the counts of 1 and 2, recover your arm on 3, and return your hand to the kickboard on 4. Exhale during the entire first 4 counts, then inhale on Counts 5 and 6 while your hand rests on the kickboard. Repeat on the count of 1 with the same arm. Continue kicking and pulling with the non-breathing-side arm.

**Success Goal** = 100 yards or meters of crawl kick and stroke

**Your Score** = (#) _____ yards or meters

## 5. Crawl Kick and Stroke With Breathing-Side Arm, Using Mask, Snorkel, and Kickboard

Don a mask and a snorkel and hold a kickboard in both hands at arm's length. Kick in 6-count cycles, beginning with the leg on your breathing side (a). After two full cycles, begin stroking with your breathing-side arm on the count of 4 (b). Pull through on the counts of 4 and 5, recover on 6, and return your hand to the kickboard on the count of 1. Inhale on Counts 5 and 6, and exhale during Counts 1 through 4. Continue kicking and pulling with the breathing-side arm.

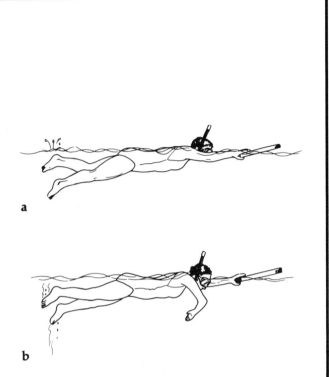

**Success Goal =**

100 yards or meters of crawl kick and stroke

**Your Score =**

(#) _____ yards or meters

## 6. Crawl Kick and Stroke With Kickboard, Mask, and Snorkel

Don a mask and a snorkel and hold a kickboard in both hands at arm's length in front of you. Kick, beginning the 6-beat count with the leg on your breathing side. After two full kick cycles, begin stroking with your non-breathing-side arm. Pull the arm through and return the hand to the board at the count of 4. Begin pulling with the breathing-side arm on the count of 4 and return the hand to the board on the count of 1; the board will float free for just an instant, as one hand returns and the other begins to pull. Stroke and kick very slowly in order to facilitate the transfer of the board from one hand to the other. Exhale on Counts 1 through 4, then inhale on Counts 5 and 6. Continue to kick and stroke for 25 yards or meters.

**Success Goal =** repeat this drill 4 times

**Your Score =** (#) _____ drill repetitions

## 7. Crawl Kick and Stroke Without Kickboard

Repeat Drill 6 without a kickboard. Imagine that the kickboard is there, though, and follow the same pattern. Stop and restart anytime you lose coordination.

**Success Goal** = 100 yards or meters of nonstop crawl kick and stroke

**Your Score** = (#) _____ yards or meters

## 8. Crawl Armstroke and Breathing, No Kick

Use goggles and a leg float. Begin in a prone glide position. Do not kick at all, but count as if you *were* kicking.

Pull with your non-breathing-side arm on Counts 1 and 2; recover it on 3; and place it back into the water, fingertips first, on 4. Start the breathing-side armstroke on 4; pull through on 5; recover on 6; and place it into the water, fingertips first, on 1. Roll your face out of the water and inhale on the count of 5, roll it back into the water on 6, and exhale the rest of the time. Keep your legs together and hold them still.

**Success Goal** =

   100 yards or meters of nonstop crawl
      armstroke

**Your Score** =

   (#) _____ yards or meters

## 9. Fully Coordinated Crawl Stroke

Wear goggles but no mask, fins, or snorkel. Begin with a prone glide, kicking in 6-beat cycles. Start the count on a kick with your breathing-side leg. Count two full cycles before beginning the armstroke.

Start the armstroke with your non-breathing-side arm. On Counts 1 and 2, leave your face down and exhale, but roll your non-breathing-side shoulder up out of the water as the arm pulls through. Keep your shoulder high but leave your face down and continue exhaling as your arm recovers and stretches forward. Roll your shoulders back through the horizontal on the count of 4, and begin the roll to your breathing side as your non-breathing-side hand enters the water, fingertips first, and the breathing-side arm begins its pull. Roll both face and shoulder out of the water, and inhale on the count of 5. Keep your breathing-side shoulder out of the water as your breathing-side arm recovers on the count of 6 and stretches forward. Roll your shoulders and face back through the horizontal on the count of 1; then begin to exhale as your breathing-side hand enters the water and your non-breathing-side arm begins its pull.

You see? It's really very easy!

**Success Goal** = 5 swims of 100 yards or meters in *correct* coordination, resting 30 seconds between swims

**Your Score** = (#) _____ swims of 100 yards or meters done correctly

## 10. Discovering Your Natural Coordination Preference

Use goggles but no other aids. Begin with the idea that you will swim lengths continuously for a period of at least 10 minutes.

Begin swimming the crawl stroke, concentrating on the correct timing of your arms, that is, one arm beginning its stroke just before the other arm enters the water. *Do not count!* Concentrate so hard on the armstroke and breathing that you forget all about your legs. Let them do whatever they want, but do not consciously hold them still. Concentrate on breathing during the last half of the pull, not on the recovery. Concentrate on the pull-push and the S-shaped arm motion, but do not think about your legs.

Alert your coach or instructor to what you are doing; ask him or her to watch your efforts sometime during the middle of the period when you are not thinking about your legs. After several observations of this sort over a period of several days, your coach or teacher should be able to tell you what arm-leg coordination is natural for you. (You probably won't believe it when you are told.)

**Success Goal** = discover your natural arm-leg coordination

**Your Score** = _____ ratio of leg kicks to arm pulls

## Crawl Stroke
## Keys to Success Checklist

You can count the number of yards you swim, but you cannot see yourself swimming except on a videotape. Expert human observers are much better at analyzing stroking ease and smoothness than the video camera, though. Have your instructor or coach study your stroke for a few lengths and evaluate it according to the checklist within Figure 1.9.

# Step 2  Crawl Stroke Turns

Swimming in a pool or another enclosed area necessitates frequent course reversals as you reach the end of the area. It is desirable to change course with a minimum expenditure of energy and minimum disruption of rhythm and swimming form. An "open turn" is such a course reversal in which your head comes above the water, allowing you to get a breath on the turn. A turn in which your head remains underwater is called a "closed turn."

## WHY IS A TURN IMPORTANT?

The open turn is the choice of most recreational and fitness swimmers for changing direction at the end of a swimming course. It is the smoothest, quickest turn that allows breathing. There are different open turns for each style of swimming. The closed turn for the crawl stroke is called a "tumble turn" because it employs a somersault motion. It is universally recognized to be the quickest turn yet discovered, and it will cut more from your competitive swimming time than any other turn. It is used by all freestyle swimmers in the Olympic Games.

## HOW TO DO A CRAWL STROKE OPEN TURN

It is essential to judge your distance from the end wall to make an open turn safely. Two options are available for judging this distance: Either raise your head slightly to look forward above the water or look for underwater turn targets. All pools designed for competitive swimming have lines on the bottom of the pool in each lane. A large cross or "T" on the bottom at the end of a lane line and a cross on the end wall are turn targets. The target on the bottom may be either 2 meters (6 feet 7 inches) or 5 feet from the wall, depending on whether the pool is designed for competition in meters or yards.

In pools not marked for competition, you must raise your head to see the end of the pool. Wearing goggles or a mask greatly facilitates judging distances underwater. With a little practice, you will be able to judge your distance from the end wall.

When about 5 feet from the wall or when over a turn target, pull through to the end of an armstroke, roll onto your side, and glide with your pulling hand resting on your thigh. Leave your bottom arm fully extended in glide position just under the surface. As your forward hand reaches the end wall, absorb the shock by placing your palm flat against the wall and allowing your elbow to bend, keeping your forearm between your head and the wall. As your elbow bends, remain on your side and tuck both knees up to your chin.

Leave your top arm pointing toward the other end as you push with your palm against the wall, raise your head sideways, inhale quickly, and use the momentum from your glide to pivot sideways so your feet come directly under you to the wall. Keep your knees tucked and lay your ear on the other arm. Bring your arm from the wall, over the water, and beside the other arm as you roll onto your face; your feet push off the wall into an underwater prone glide position. Glide until your speed slows to equal your swimming speed, then begin stroking for the next length.

If the pool design is such that you can take hold of the end wall, either by the edge of an overflow trough or by a low coping, you should grasp the end, pull yourself into the wall, and press downward to accelerate your pivot. Pulling yourself into the wall is faster and will keep you closer for a better push-off.

The entire process should have a rhythm; you should be able to count it off with the key words "pull, touch, pivot, arm over, push, glide." The turn should be smooth and fluid, without hesitation (see Figure 2.1).

*Figure 2.1  Keys to Success:*
        ***Crawl Stroke***
        ***Open Turn***

**Preparation
Phase**

1. Judge distance to wall to determine which hand will make contact \_\_\_\_

**Execution
Phase**

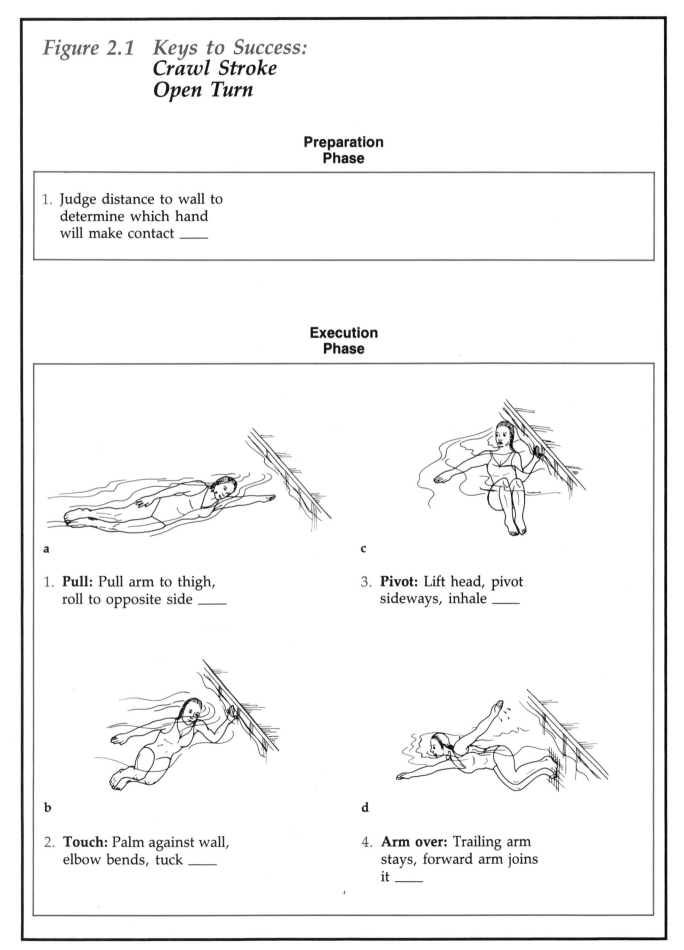

**a**

1. **Pull:** Pull arm to thigh, roll to opposite side \_\_\_\_

**b**

2. **Touch:** Palm against wall, elbow bends, tuck \_\_\_\_

**c**

3. **Pivot:** Lift head, pivot sideways, inhale \_\_\_\_

**d**

4. **Arm over:** Trailing arm stays, forward arm joins it \_\_\_\_

5. **Stay tucked:** Feet on wall _____

7. **Glide:** Slow to swimming speed _____

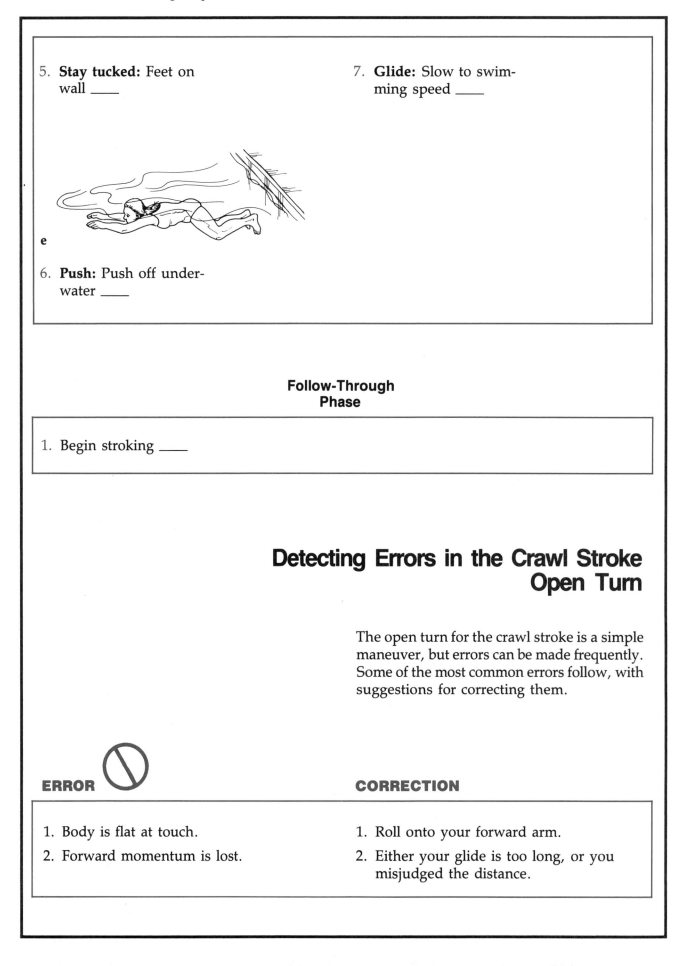

e

6. **Push:** Push off underwater _____

**Follow-Through
Phase**

1. Begin stroking _____

# Detecting Errors in the Crawl Stroke Open Turn

The open turn for the crawl stroke is a simple maneuver, but errors can be made frequently. Some of the most common errors follow, with suggestions for correcting them.

**ERROR**

**CORRECTION**

1. Body is flat at touch.

2. Forward momentum is lost.

1. Roll onto your forward arm.

2. Either your glide is too long, or you misjudged the distance.

**ERROR** ⊘

**CORRECTION**

| ERROR | CORRECTION |
|---|---|
| 3. Turn finishes too far from wall, resulting in poor push. | 3. Bend your elbow as you touch. |
| 4. You push off from wall with arm in air. | 4. Release the wall before your feet touch, and delay the push-off until your arms are together. |
| 5. Body spins horizontally. | 5. Stay on your side during the pivot. |
| 6. You remain underwater on glide. | 6. Inhale more deeply or keep the push-off shallow. |
| 7. You push off on the surface. | 7. Allow your body to sink before you push off, and aim slightly downhill. |
| 8. You begin stroking too soon. | 8. Glide for a count of 3 or 4. |

## HOW TO DO A CRAWL STROKE TUMBLE TURN

Because this turn is used primarily for competition, it will be assumed that turn targets (large Ts or crosses) are designed into the pool floors and end walls in sizes and at distances prescribed by competitive swimming rules. (See the *United States Swimming Rules and Regulations* or the *National Collegiate Athletic Association Men's and Women's Swimming and Diving Rules*.) Swim the crawl stroke toward the end of the pool. As your head passes over the turn target on the floor of the pool, finish the arm pull in progress but leave the arm back so your hand is at your thigh. Pull with the next arm and leave that hand beside the other thigh. By this time your head should be about 3 to 4 feet from the wall.

As your second hand reaches your thigh, turn both straight arms so your palms are down, then quickly lift both legs together and drive them downward sharply (large dolphin kick) as you bend forward at your hips and drive your head down to initiate a forward somersault. Press your hands and arms downward and scoop forward to lift your hips. As your upper torso reaches the vertical position, turn your head to one side and quickly tuck both knees to accelerate the speed of the somersault. Your arms should complete their scooping motion with your hands at about ear level. Your forearms then rotate so your palms are facing upward beside your ears.

As your feet move ahead of your body, you will be lying nearly on your back underwater (slightly on one side) in tuck position with your feet against the wall. Your head turn during the half somersault causes you to look at one hand. Push upward with that hand to start turning your body into a prone position, then initiate a strong push from the wall. As you leave the wall and roll into prone position, extend both arms forward and streamline your body. Glide underwater and turn your fingertips upward to reach the surface as your glide slows to top swimming speed. Begin stroking, but do not take a breath until the second or third armstroke (see Figure 2.2).

*Figure 2.2  Keys to Success:*
**Crawl Stroke**
**Tumble Turn**

**Preparation**
**Phase**

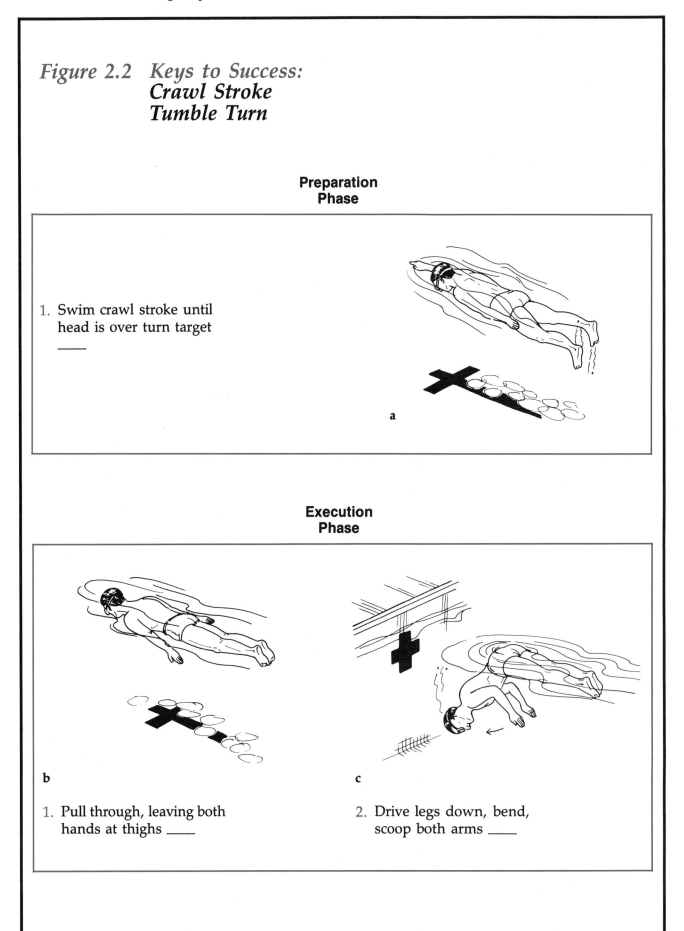

1. Swim crawl stroke until
   head is over turn target
   ____

a

**Execution**
**Phase**

b

1. Pull through, leaving both
   hands at thighs ____

c

2. Drive legs down, bend,
   scoop both arms ____

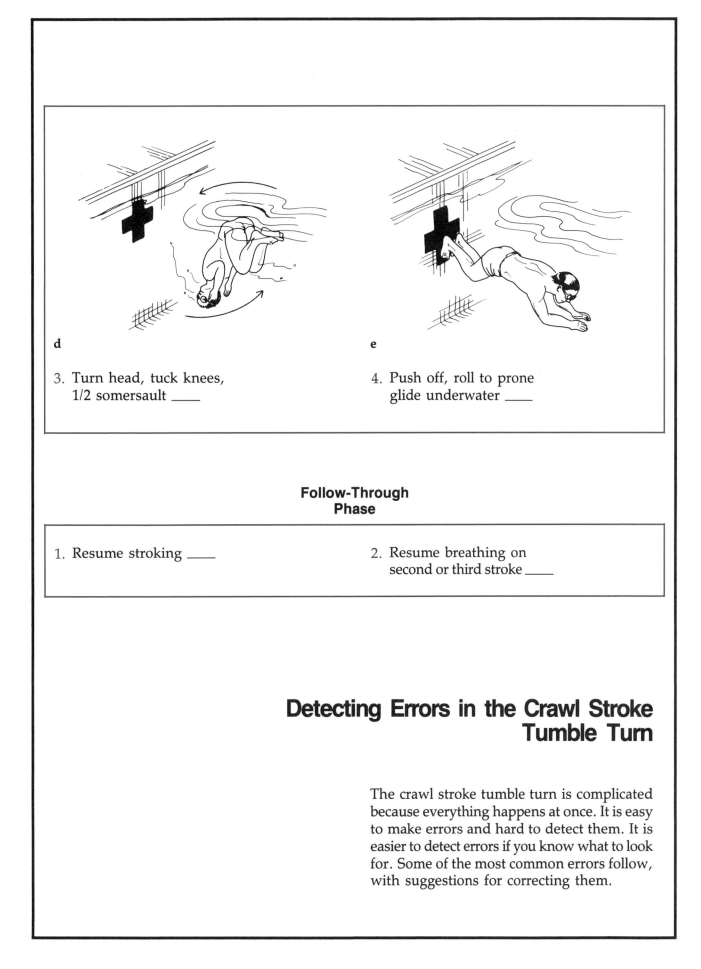

d

3. Turn head, tuck knees,
   1/2 somersault ____

e

4. Push off, roll to prone
   glide underwater ____

**Follow-Through
Phase**

1. Resume stroking ____

2. Resume breathing on
   second or third stroke ____

# Detecting Errors in the Crawl Stroke Tumble Turn

The crawl stroke tumble turn is complicated because everything happens at once. It is easy to make errors and hard to detect them. It is easier to detect errors if you know what to look for. Some of the most common errors follow, with suggestions for correcting them.

**ERROR**

**CORRECTION**

1. You misjudge distance from wall.

2. You can't get over in somersault.

3. Your somersault is slow.

4. You hit your heels on wall.

1. Practice, practice, practice.

2. Emphasize a straight-leg dolphin kick.

3. Scoop arms harder, tuck knees more quickly.

4. Tuck tighter or start farther from wall.

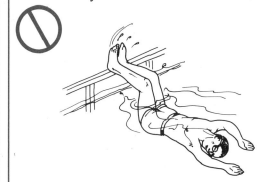

5. You are flat on your back before pushing off.

6. You get your nose full of water.

5. Turn your head while scooping with your arms.

6. Make a short, forcible exhalation in midturn.

# Crawl Stroke Open Turn Drills

## 1. Open Crawl Turn, Push, and Glide

Don swimming goggles. Stand at arm's length from a pool wall in water 3 to 4 feet deep. Turn your side to the wall and extend both arms out to your sides. Grasp the edge of the gutter or the coping with one hand and lay your other arm, pointing slightly downward, on the water. Sink down until your chin is on the water. Lean your head away from the wall and lay your ear on your outstretched arm.

Continue to hold the edge as you tuck both knees and place both feet against the wall just under the surface (a). You should now be floating on your side, tucked, with one hand on the wall to steady you and your feet against the wall. Keeping your knees tucked, *do not push off* but bring your hand quickly from the wall *over* the water and place it beside the forward hand (b). This movement will turn you face-down as you float.

Lift your chin so you are looking straight forward underwater, and now push off slightly downhill (if you do not raise your chin before pushing off, the water will push your goggles off). Streamline your whole body. Stretch your arms and legs and point your toes. Turn your hands upward to guide you to the surface about three body lengths from the wall. Swim two strokes of the crawl stroke and stop. Repeat, starting with your other side to the wall.

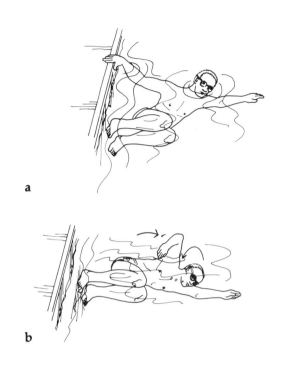

**Success Goal =**

10 push-offs in good form on each side

**Your Score =**

(#) _____ push-offs on each side

## 2. *Approach to Open Crawl Turn*

Don swimming goggles. Stand in water about 4 feet deep, facing the end wall of the pool from about 6 feet away. Stretch both arms toward the wall and bend over to put your chin at water level.

Push off gently into a prone glide toward the wall. As soon as your feet leave the bottom, begin a crawl stroke pull with your left arm. As your left arm pulls, roll onto your right side. Stop the left arm pull when your hand reaches your thigh, then do a side glide into the wall. Remain on your side as you grasp the rim of the overflow trough, tuck your knees quickly, and pull yourself toward the wall.

Drop your feet directly under your body and complete the open turn as in the previous drill. Repeat the turn on your left side.

**Success Goal =** 10 open turns on each side

**Your Score =** (#) _____ open turns on each side

## 3. *Open Crawl Turn With Free Pivot*

Don swimming goggles. From a position about 30 feet from the end of the pool, swim the crawl stroke toward the end. Judge your distance from the end either by lifting your head momentarily and looking forward over the water or by using the turn targets on the pool bottom.

Swim into an open turn but do not maintain a hold on the pool edge during the pivot. Use your forward hand to pull quickly on the wall and to *initiate* the pivot. As soon as your feet are moving under you, however, release the wall and bring your arm over the water as your body *floats* through the pivot. By the time your feet touch the wall, your arms should already be in position for the push-off. You can even initiate the push-off a split second before your feet touch. The result of this free-floating pivot should be a much smoother turn without hesitation just before the push-off. The turn should have a more fluid rhythm.

**Success Goal** = 10 free-pivot turns on each side

**Your Score** = (#) _____ free-pivot turns on each side

## 4. *Open Turns on a Flat Wall*

Don swimming goggles. Swim the crawl stroke toward the end of the pool. Judge your distance, and glide into an open turn but do not grasp the edge. Keep your hand just below the surface of the water and place your palm flat against the pool wall. Take up the shock of hitting the wall by pressure on your forward arm, but allow your elbow to bend until your entire forearm is flat against the pool wall. Keep your arm directly in front of your head.

As your head touches your forearm, push gently down and away on the wall to initiate your pivot. Use just enough pressure on your forward hand to initiate the pivot without pushing yourself so far from the wall that you cannot get a good push-off. As soon as you begin the pivot, bring your forward hand over the water, float through the pivot, and push off.

Repeat on the other side.

**Success Goal** = obtain a solid push-off on 10 consecutive turns on each side

**Your Score** = (#) _____ consecutive solid push-offs on each side

# Crawl Stroke Tumble Turn Drills

## 1. Half-Somersault Drill

Wear a nose clip and goggles. Perform the drill in about 4 feet of water, away from any wall.

Swim four strokes of the crawl stroke. Stop one arm down at your side, pull through with the other arm, and stop with both arms at your sides. Rotate your arms so your palms face downward. Keeping your legs straight, arch your back slightly to lift both feet to the surface. Then quickly and forcibly drive both straight legs downward as you bend sharply at your hips to drive your head straight toward the bottom of the pool. Use both arms to scoop forcibly downward and forward to pull your head under your body and to lift your hips over your head (a).

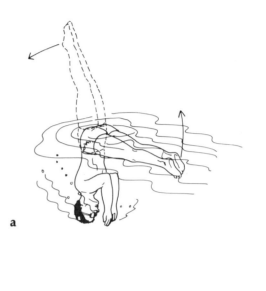

a

As your torso passes the vertical position, keep your legs straight and snap your hips open sharply to throw your legs forward over the water past your body, putting you flat on your back at the surface and heading in the opposite direction (b). As your feet splash into the water, place both hands palms up beside your ears.

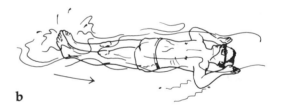

b

**Success Goal =**

10 half somersaults in open water, correctly executed

**Your Score =**

(#) _____ half somersaults

## 2. Half Somersaults to a Wall

Wear a nose clip and goggles. Start swimming about 20 feet from the end wall in water about 4 feet deep.

Do a half somersault as described in the previous drill, but be sure you start your somersault when your head is still about 4 feet short of the turn target. Keep your legs straight throughout the somersault. By streamlining your body, try to coast into the wall feetfirst on your back.

Gauge your distance from the wall carefully and repeat the somersault again and again, initiating your turn just a little closer to the wall each time, until you can complete the somersault with your feet about 1 foot from the wall and can drift into the wall forcibly. Use caution to prevent hitting your heels on the wall as your feet enter the water.

**Success Goal =** 10 consecutive trials in which you glide into the wall forcibly

**Your Score =** (#) _____ consecutive trials with solid wall contact

## 3. Tumble Turn With Twist

Repeat the preceding drill, but as you bend at your hips, turn your head to one side and keep it turned as your legs fly forward. The object is to add enough twist to the somersault so that you are on your side as your feet contact the wall. Try turning your head in each direction until you decide which side works better for you.

**Success Goal =** 10 consecutive turns in which your feet contact the wall while you are lying on your side

**Your Score =** (#) _____ consecutive turns on your side

## 4. Adding Knee Bend to the Crawl Stroke Tumble Turn

Use a nose clip and goggles. Perform a turn just as you did in Drill 3, but as soon as your body passes the vertical position in the somersault, tuck your knees sharply and try to drift into the wall in a tuck position.

Carefully move a little closer with each trial until your feet are in contact with the wall at the completion of the somersault and no time is needed for drifting in. Use the turn target on the bottom of the pool to help you gauge your distance from the wall. Push off, glide, and resume stroking after each turn.

**Success Goal =** 10 consecutive tuck tumble turns in which your feet are against the wall on completion of the somersault

**Your Score =** (#) _____ consecutive successful turns

## 5. Crawl Stroke Tumble Turns Without Nose Clip

Wear goggles but do not use a nose clip. Practice tumble turns. As your body tumbles past the vertical position, exhale sharply through your nose just until your feet hit the wall. Only a momentary exhalation is needed; save the rest of your air until you exhale on your second or third armstroke.

**Success Goal** = 10 turns without getting water in your nose

**Your Score** = (#) _____ comfortable turns

## 6. Crawl Stroke Tumble Turns for Speed

Tie a line across the pool about 3 feet above the water and 15 or 16 feet from the end wall. Competitive pool backstroke warning flags work well, but try to lower them to 3 feet above water.

Practice swimming into tumble turns from about 30 or 35 feet from the wall. Increase your swimming speed each time until you can enter the turn at top speed and complete the turn smoothly.

Then get a helper with a hand-held stopwatch or digital timer. Have your timer start the watch when your head passes under the line as you swim toward the wall, and stop the watch when your head passes under the line as you come from the turn.

**Success Goal** = 5 consecutive time trials under 9 seconds

**Your Score** = (#) _____ consecutive trials under 9 seconds

# Crawl Stroke Turns
# Keys to Success Checklists

Mechanical performance of the crawl stroke open turn can be learned by successive repetitions, but smoothness, fluidity, and rhythmical performance must be evaluated by an expert eye. Have your coach or instructor evaluate both your open and your tumble turns for the crawl stroke according to the criteria listed in Figures 2.1 and 2.2, respectively.

# *Step 3*  Improving the Back Crawl Kick

Early in your basic swimming training, you learned to kick your feet in an up-and-down fluttering motion while floating on your back. That was a rudimentary back crawl kick. Now it is time to perfect that kick in preparation for learning the back crawl stroke. Your early efforts in kicking helped build your confidence and contribute to your safety in the water. Now this step will build the foundation for learning a very popular competitive swimming stroke.

## WHY IS THE BACK CRAWL KICK IMPORTANT?

The backstroke kick is an inverted version of the crawl stroke kick, but done somewhat deeper. What contributes the greatest propulsion is the forward motion in which the shin and the top of the foot press on the water. When you are swimming prone, the crawl stroke kick allows this forward (downward) movement only from the top of the water to the kick's maximum depth of about 15 inches. When you swim on your back, however, you can use a deeper kick that allows the more efficient forward (upward) motion to be made through a greater distance. The result? The backstroke kick is deeper and provides more propulsive force than the crawl kick.

## HOW TO DO THE BACK CRAWL KICK

From a back float position with arms extended overhead, begin an alternate up-and-down kicking. Lay your head back until both ears are underwater. Keep your hips up; avoid dropping them into a partial sitting position. Relax your ankles completely so your foot flops as the water pressure forces it into the hooked position on the downward motion and the pointed position on the upward motion. Relaxed ankles result in your feet assuming a somewhat pigeon-toed position. Keep each knee straight on the downward portion of the kick, and drop your foot about 20 inches below the surface.

As you begin the upward thrust from your hip, allow your knee to bend moderately (about 60 degrees below the surface of the water). Keep the bend stable as you continue to kick your whole leg upward from the hip joint, pushing up and back with your shin and the top of your foot. When your knee is about 3 inches under the surface, stop the upward motion of your thigh and straighten your knee so the foot spoons water up. The feeling is that of flipping water up and back with the top of your foot. However, you are only raising a mound of surface turbulence without actually splashing. As soon as your knee straightens, start your leg downward from the hip again. Continue alternate upward thrusts (see Figure 3.1).

*Figure 3.1  Keys to Success:*
    ***Back Crawl Kick***

**Preparation
Phase**

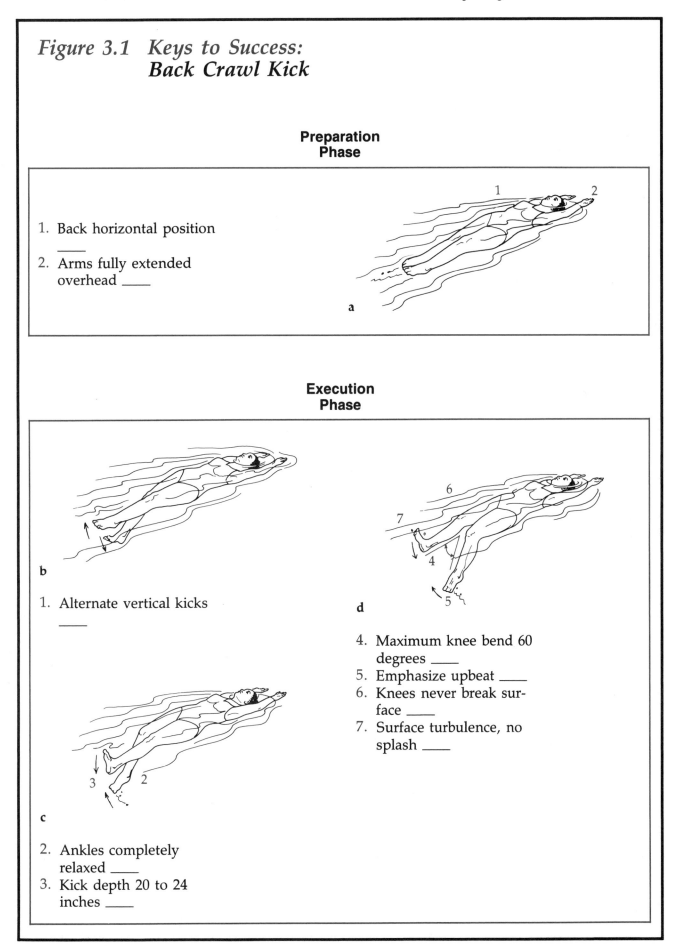

1. Back horizontal position
____

2. Arms fully extended
overhead ____

a

**Execution
Phase**

b

1. Alternate vertical kicks
____

d

4. Maximum knee bend 60
degrees ____
5. Emphasize upbeat ____
6. Knees never break sur-
face ____
7. Surface turbulence, no
splash ____

c

2. Ankles completely
relaxed ____
3. Kick depth 20 to 24
inches ____

**Follow-Through
Phase**

1. Continued rhythmical
   upthrusts _____

2. Smooth forward
   progress _____

# Detecting Errors in the Back Crawl Kick

The back crawl kick is relatively easy to do, but some errors are commonly seen. The following list suggests corrections for the common mistakes.

**ERROR**                                        **CORRECTION**

1. Legs splash.                                  1. Keep knees, feet submerged.
2. Kick gives no power.                          2. Limit knee bend to 60 degrees, check ankle flexion.
3. Body bent in sitting position.                3. Lie back, lift hips.

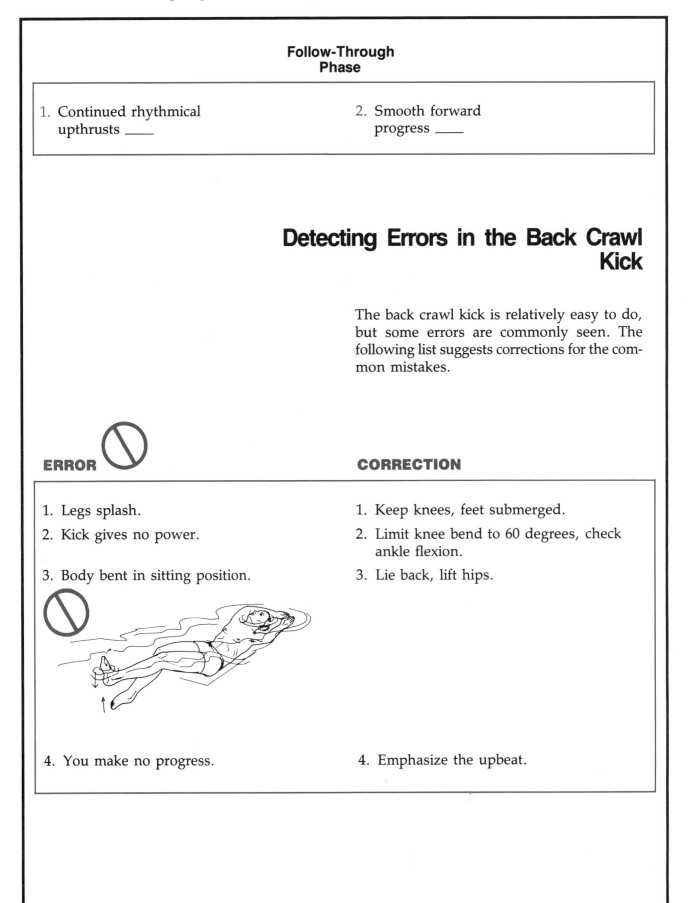

4. You make no progress.                         4. Emphasize the upbeat.

# Back Crawl Kick Drills

## 1. Backstroke Kick, Kickboard at Hips

Goggles are optional; a nose clip is not necessary. Start in water of standing depth. Hold a kickboard lengthwise in front of you with both arms on top of the board and your fingers grasping the far end.

Lie back and press your hips up under the board. Keep your arms straight so the far end of the kickboard remains at about midthigh. Kick pool lengths as described, keeping your knees and feet underwater and your hips pressed up under the board.

*CAUTION: Be alert when approaching the end of the pool: Do not bump your head.*

### Success Goal =

100 yards or meters of backstroke kick
  with hips up and no splash

### Your Score =

(#) _____ yards or meters of backstroke kick

## 2. Back Crawl Kick, Board Overhead

Goggles are optional. Avoid getting water in your nose by inhaling through your mouth and exhaling through your nose. If it is practical, use either backstroke turn flags or competitive swimming lane lines to help judge your distance from the end of the pool. Backstroke turn flags cross the pool 15 feet or 5 meters from the end wall. Competitive swimming lane lines have 15 feet or 5 meters of distinctive colored floats at each end.

Lie on your back in the water with both arms stretched straight overhead. Hold the trailing edge of a kickboard in both hands. Keep your head back between your arms so both ears are underwater, and keep your hips up, as you kick pool lengths. Keep your knees and feet underwater but try to raise a mound of turbulence above your feet.

**Success Goal =** 2 repetitions of 100 yards or meters of backstroke kick in good form,
  with 2 minutes rest between repetitions

**Your Score =** (#) _____ repetitions of 100 yards or meters in good form

### 3. Backstroke Kick, Hands Clasped

Use goggles and, if practical, use backstroke turn lines and lane lines. Control the problem of water getting into your nose by exhaling through your nose and inhaling through your mouth.

Extend both arms above your head, cross your forearms, and turn your hands so your palms face inward. Clasp your hands with palms together and fingers intertwined. Press your arms tight over your ears.

Hold that position as you lie on your back and practice the backstroke kick. Keep your head in line with your body, ears staying underwater. Keep your hips up and your feet and knees underwater. Emphasize the upward spooning flip of the feet. Try to raise a consistent mound of turbulence above your feet; kick up *to* the surface but not *through* it. At each end of the pool, take hold of the pool edge, turn, push off, and then return to the clasped-hands position.

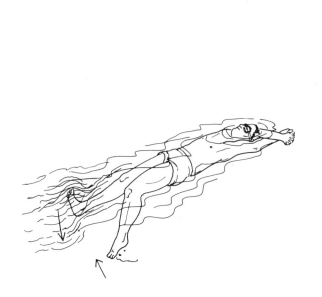

**Success Goal =**

3 repetitions of 100 yards or meters of backstroke kick with a 2-minute rest between repetitions

**Your Score =**

(#) _____ repetitions of 100 yards or meters

### 4. Backstroke Kick Against the Wall

Goggles are optional. You need a stopwatch, a timer, or a clock with a sweep second hand.

At the shallow end of the pool, stretch both arms overhead and lie in the water on your back with both hands against the pool end wall. Have someone time you upon giving a start command. Begin the backstroke kick on the command. Kick continuously, pushing against the wall for 1 minute. Keep your head back, your hips up, your feet and knees underwater. Concentrate on pushing the water back and up with your lower legs and the tops of your feet.

**Success Goal =** 3 repetitions of kicking for 1 minute, with a 30-second rest between repetitions

**Your Score =** (#) _____ 1-minute kicking repetitions

# Back Crawl Kick
# Keys to Success Checklist

You have attained goals of distance and time while kicking on your back, but how smoothly, how well, and how powerfully you kick determines the quality of your kick. Have your coach or teacher evaluate your back crawl kick qualitatively using the Keys to Success within Figure 3.1 as a checklist.

# *Step 4* **Back Crawl Armstroke**

The back crawl armstroke is like no other armstroke. It only vaguely resembles the crawl stroke arm motion in that it uses an alternate, overarm recovery. In every other respect, it is completely different.

## WHY IS THE BACK CRAWL ARMSTROKE IMPORTANT?

The back crawl armstroke is a major component of one of the so-called standard competitive swimming strokes. Of more importance, though, is the concept it introduces to the swimmer's repertoire: It is the only alternating armstroke used while swimming on the back.

## HOW TO DO THE BACK CRAWL ARMSTROKE

Start with a glide on your back, both arms stretched overhead with palms facing outward. Roll slightly onto one side and drop one shoulder a little deeper into the water. Rotate your lower arm outward from the shoulder so your palm faces downward, as if you were reaching behind you to grasp the edge of the pool. Now bend your wrist forward sharply to put your palm in position to press directly backward toward your feet. Leave your elbow as high (as far forward) as possible while you begin to pull with your hand and forearm. Bend your elbow to bring the forearm into position to press directly backward toward your feet.

As your forearm attains pulling position perpendicular to your body, straighten your wrist again. At this point your forearm and hand should be about 12 inches under the water and parallel to the surface. Your elbow should be bent about 90 degrees, and your upper arm should have moved very little from the shoulder. You are now in position to exert maximum force directly backward against the water. Leave your elbow bent as you pull

directly toward your feet with your entire arm. Your hand and forearm should rise slightly toward the surface as you pull, your hand about 4 inches deep as it passes your shoulder. As your arm passes your shoulder, begin to straighten your elbow and relax your wrist. The water pressure will begin to bend your hand back at the wrist. Keep it perpendicular to the line of thrust as long as possible.

As your arm nears full extension, rotate the entire arm from the shoulder to a palm-down position and press downward, flipping your hand downward as it passes your thigh. Use this downward hand pressure to help you roll away from that side and elevate that shoulder above the water for the arm recovery. Keep your elbow straight but allow your wrist to be perfectly relaxed as you lift your arm from the water palm down. If your wrist is totally relaxed, your hand will flop to a position at approximately a right angle to your arm. Raise your straight arm directly upward through a vertical position. As your arm passes shoulder height on its recovery phase, rotate your entire arm from the shoulder so your fingertips point outward, away from your body. Stretch your arm as far forward as possible as you roll onto that side again and place your hand in the water, palm down, ready to start the next pull.

The opposite arm follows exactly the same pattern, beginning its pull as you roll toward that side to effect the recovery of the first arm. Your arms should be in direct opposition to each other at all times: When one arm is in midpull, the other should be in midrecovery; when one arm is finishing a pull, the other should be entering the water.

Keep your hips up and your head back so both ears remain underwater. Do not allow your head to roll as your shoulders roll. Look steadily and directly at the ceiling (see Figure 4.1).

*Figure 4.1  Keys to Success:*
*Back Crawl*
*Armstroke*

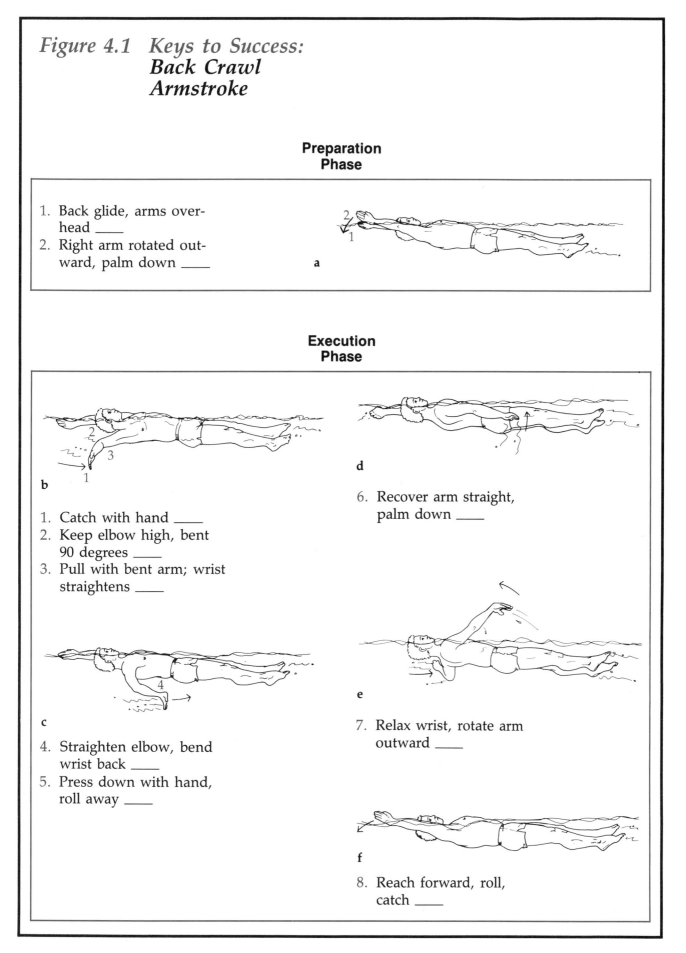

**Preparation Phase**

1. Back glide, arms over-
   head ____
2. Right arm rotated out-
   ward, palm down ____

a

**Execution Phase**

b

1. Catch with hand ____
2. Keep elbow high, bent
   90 degrees ____
3. Pull with bent arm; wrist
   straightens ____

c

4. Straighten elbow, bend
   wrist back ____
5. Press down with hand,
   roll away ____

d

6. Recover arm straight,
   palm down ____

e

7. Relax wrist, rotate arm
   outward ____

f

8. Reach forward, roll,
   catch ____

**Follow-Through
Phase**

1. Move arms exactly in opposition ____

2. Continue steady, even rhythm ____

# Detecting Errors in the Back Crawl Armstroke

Several errors are common in performing the back crawl armstroke because one arm is held straight while the other bends. Some of the common errors follow with suggestions for their elimination.

**ERROR**

**CORRECTION**

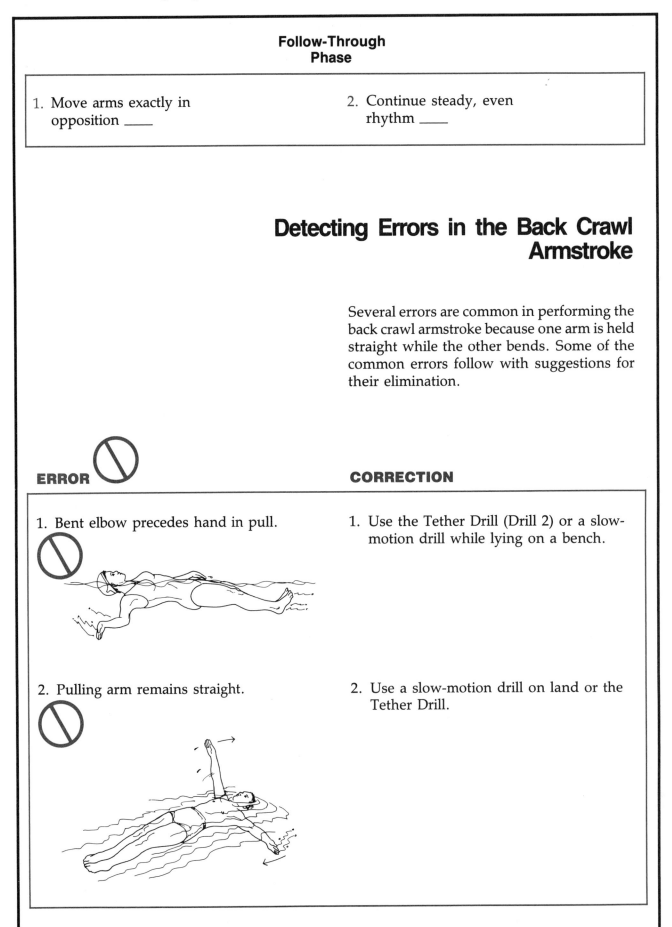

1. Bent elbow precedes hand in pull.

1. Use the Tether Drill (Drill 2) or a slow-motion drill while lying on a bench.

2. Pulling arm remains straight.

2. Use a slow-motion drill on land or the Tether Drill.

**ERROR**                                    **CORRECTION**

3. Pulling arm is too deep.                  3. Bend your elbow more.

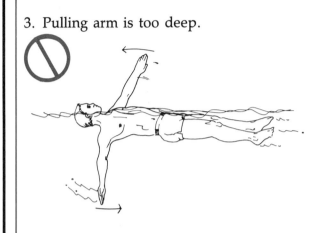

4. Recovering arm bends.                      4. Watch your arm as it moves.

5. Hand overreaches, entering directly        5. Roll your shoulders more; keep arm
   overhead.                                     slightly out from body.

6. Arm catches up to other at hips.           6. In slow motion, concentrate on opposi-
                                                 tion of arms.

7. Head rolls.                                7. ''Tie your nose'' to the ceiling.

# Back Crawl Armstroke Drills

## 1. Mental Imaging Drill

This drill is directed toward achieving the correct high-elbow arm-and-hand position at the start of the back crawl armstroke pull. Close your eyes and imagine yourself standing in a ditch with your arms at your sides. The ditch is only slightly wider than your body, and the sides rise above the top of your head. Your challenge is to get your shoulders and torso above the sides of the ditch by placing your hands over the top on both sides and pressing yourself up.

Your eyes still closed, stretch your arms above your head and imagine yourself trying this in two ways: (a) by keeping your elbows pointed down and pulling; and (b) by pressing with your elbows bent 90 degrees, your forearms and hands pointing forward, and keeping your elbows as high as possible to get them above your hands as soon as possible. Which method would be more successful? If you pick the second, you are correct.

Now think back to the moment you first began to press, elbows high, forearms and hands pointing forward. Imagine yourself floating in the water, rolled slightly to one side, reaching forward with one arm to catch the water and press it back toward your feet. Your arm should be in the same position as when you started to lift yourself from the ditch: elbow high and bent 90 degrees.

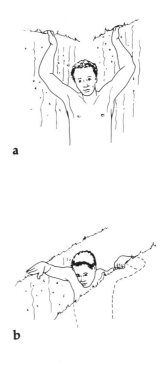

a

b

**Success Goal =**

ability to place your arm and hand in the correct position for the back crawl armstroke

**Your Score =**

_____ achieved correct position (your judgment; yes or no?)

## 2. Tether Drill, Supported

In water 4 feet deep, wear a high-buoyancy float belt. Tie a slipknot in the end of a 6- to 8-foot piece of surgical tubing, shock cord, or any line. Tie one end of the cord to a ladder, a lane line anchor, or another stable object. Put the slipknot around one ankle to float on your back tethered 2 or 3 feet from the wall.

Keep your feet together and go through the motions of the back crawl armstroke in very slow motion. Do not pull hard, but study arm, hand, and body positions at each point in the armstroke.

**Success Goal =** 10 minutes of slow-motion, studied pulling

**Your Score =** (#) ____ minutes of studied pulling

## 3. Touch-and-Go Back Crawl Arm Drill

Use a leg float between your knees. Float on your back with both arms stretched overhead. Roll partially onto your right side and pull your right arm through a backstroke arm motion. Leave your left arm stretched overhead as you roll partially onto your left side and recover your right arm. When both arms are again stretched overhead, glide for a moment in back glide position. Roll partially onto your left side and pull through with your left arm. Roll to the right for the left-arm recovery while your right arm remains stretched overhead.

Continue alternating arm pulls, completing each arm pull and gliding before beginning the next arm pull. In effect, one hand must touch the other overhead before it can go (thus, ''touch and go''). Concentrate on the correct arm position during each pull.

**Success Goal =** 100 yards or meters using correct arm motions in touch-and-go stroking

**Your Score =** (#) ____ yards or meters of correct touch and go

## 4. Pull-and-Glide Back Crawl Arm Drill

Put a leg float between your knees and stretch into back glide position. Roll onto your right side and pull through a backstroke arm pull with your right arm. As you finish the pull, roll onto your left side and stop with your right hand resting on your thigh. Glide for a count of 4 on your extended left arm, then pull with your left arm as you recover your right arm. At the end of the pull, leave your left hand on your thigh as you roll onto your right side. Glide on your right arm for a count of 4.

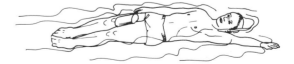

Continue, alternately pulling and gliding, but keep your arms always in exact opposition to each other. Remember: straight-arm vertical recovery, bent-arm horizontal pull.

**Success Goal =**

100 yards or meters of correct pull-and-glide stroke

**Your Score =**

(#) _____ yards or meters of pull and glide

## 5. Back Crawl Arm Pull, Counting

Place a leg float between your knees and start in a back glide position, arms stretched overhead. Begin a steady, rhythmical back crawl armstroke with no glide or hesitation. Keep your arms directly opposed to each other throughout the stroke.

After two or three strokes, begin counting in 6-beat rhythm. Say ''one'' as your right hand strikes the water on its entry overhead, and say ''two'' and ''three'' as it pulls. Say ''four'' as your left hand strikes the water on entry, and say ''five'' and ''six'' as it pulls.

Continue counting the 6-beat rhythm as you swim. If you get off-count, stop, slow down, and begin again.

**Success Goal =** 100 yards or meters of continuous, rhythmical 6-beat back crawl armstroke without losing count

**Your Score =** (#) _____ yards or meters of continuous back crawl armstroke

## 6. Back Crawl Head Position Drill

Use a leg float between your knees. From a back glide position, begin a steady back crawl armstroke. Concentrate on holding your head absolutely still as your shoulders rotate from side to side. Imagine that your nose is tied with a string to a track in the ceiling and cannot turn to the side. Use your head as an anchor to steady the entire back crawl armstroke. Turn your head only if you need to look back to find the pool end wall for safety. Otherwise, try to gauge your distance from the end wall by using the backstroke turn flags or

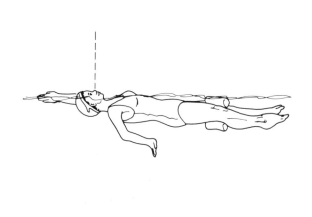

the color change in the competitive lane line floats. Coast in when you think you are close.

**Success Goal =**

100 yards or meters of back crawl armstroke in which your head remains rock steady

**Your Score =**

(#) _____ yards or meters of head-steady back crawl armstroke

# Back Crawl Armstroke Keys to Success Checklist

The swimming distance required in each of the drills is calculated to give you minimal proficiency in the objective. Qualitative judgments are necessary to assess your smoothness, relaxation, and rhythm. Have your coach or teacher complete the checklist within Figure 4.1 to assess your skill.

# *Step 5* **Coordinating the Back Crawl Stroke**

The back crawl kick and the back crawl armstroke must be finely coordinated to produce the back crawl stroke. This stroke is so named because it resembles the crawl stroke in its alternating overarm recovery and alternating vertical kicking movements. In competitive swimming circles, it is often referred to simply as the "backstroke," but this can be misleading because there is another backstroke, the elementary backstroke that you probably learned in your basic swimming training.

## WHY IS THE BACK CRAWL STROKE IMPORTANT?

The importance of the back crawl stroke stems from its use as one of the four competitive swimming strokes recognized by all competitive swimming governing bodies. In competitive swimming the term *backstroke* describes any swimming motion performed in the supine position. Because the back crawl is the fastest of these, it is the stroke that is universally used. The competitive swimming rule books have only one rule governing the execution of the "backstroke": "Swimmers shall push off on their backs and continue swimming on their backs throughout the race" (National Collegiate Athletic Association, 1988). That definition allows considerable leeway in execution, and coaches often disagree on the exact execution of the "correct" (read "fastest") backstroke.

The specific stroke in this text has led one swimmer to two national championship performances. One advantage of swimming the back crawl stroke is that your nose and mouth are free at all times, allowing you to breathe at will. Its biggest disadvantage lies in the fact that you cannot see where you are going.

## HOW TO COORDINATE THE BACK CRAWL STROKE

Begin the back crawl stroke in a back glide position with both arms stretched overhead, palms facing outward. Keep your hips up as you begin the back crawl kick. Starting with your left foot, count the upthrust of each foot in a series of 6-beat cycles. Hold your head in normal alignment with your body, your chin up and both ears submerged; do not allow your head to roll from side to side as you swim.

On the third count of 1, roll to the right and extend your right arm to catch the water for a pull. Use the armstroke exactly as described in Step 4, pulling through on the kick-counts of 2, 3, and 4. As you finish your pull on 4, roll to the left and extend your left arm for the left-arm catch. Pull with your left arm during the counts of 5 and 6, as you recover your right arm through the vertical. Finish the pull of your left arm on the count of 1, as you roll to the right and your right arm enters the water for the next catch.

Keep your arms in diametrically opposed positions as you pull with one and recover the other, and continue the cycle rhythmically. Be sure your right hand enters the water exactly on the 1-count and your left hand enters exactly on the 4-count. Keep your head steady and your hips up (see Figure 5.1). Though your nose and mouth are free to breathe at any time, you should develop the habit of exhaling through your nose during one arm pull and inhaling through your mouth during the other.

## *Figure 5.1  Keys to Success:*
### *Back Crawl Stroke*

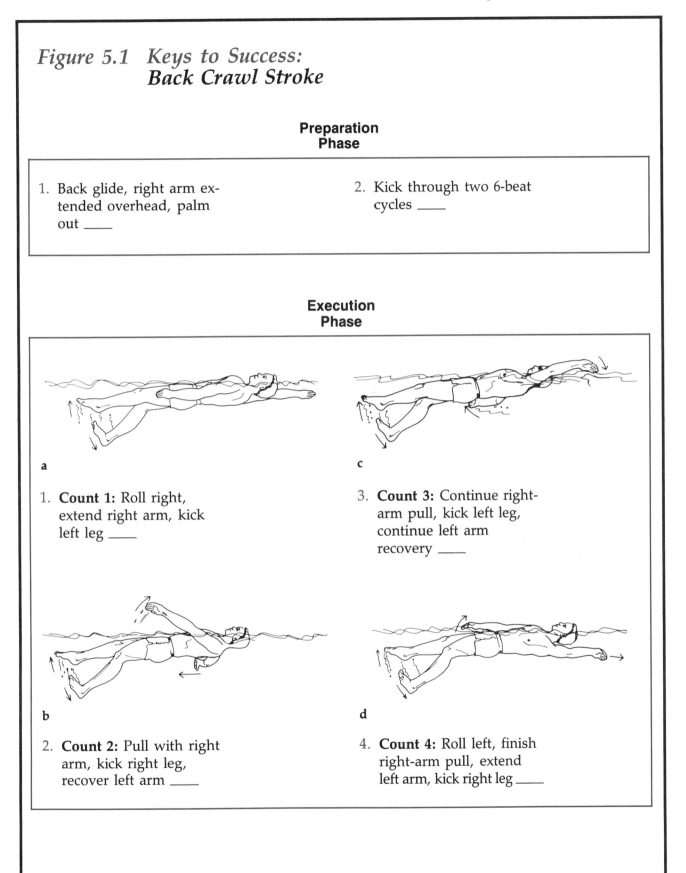

**Preparation
Phase**

1. Back glide, right arm extended overhead, palm out _____

2. Kick through two 6-beat cycles _____

**Execution
Phase**

**a**

1. **Count 1:** Roll right, extend right arm, kick left leg _____

**b**

2. **Count 2:** Pull with right arm, kick right leg, recover left arm _____

**c**

3. **Count 3:** Continue right-arm pull, kick left leg, continue left arm recovery _____

**d**

4. **Count 4:** Roll left, finish right-arm pull, extend left arm, kick right leg _____

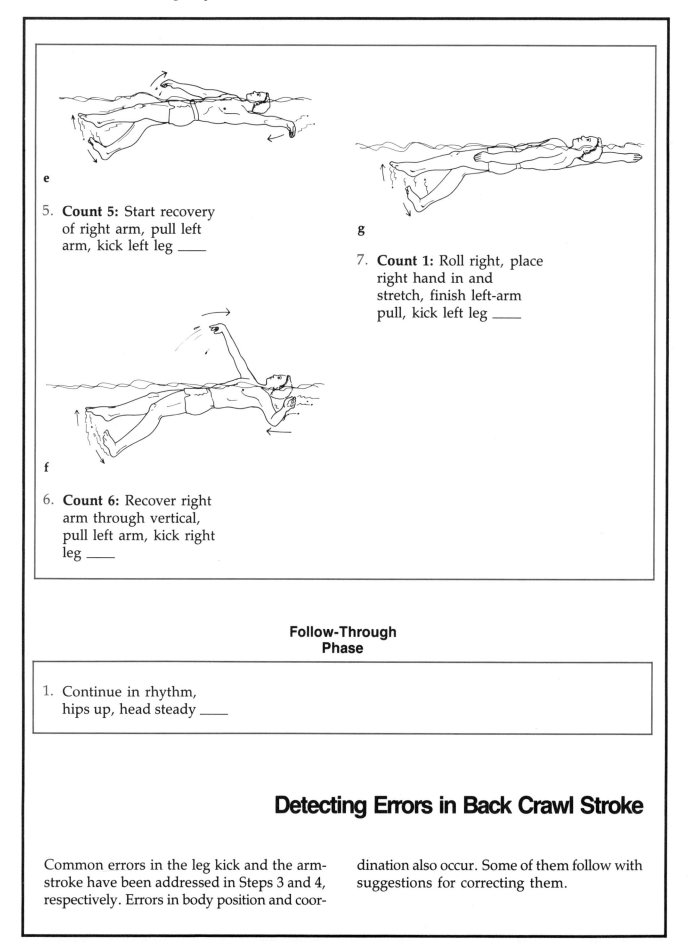

5. **Count 5:** Start recovery of right arm, pull left arm, kick left leg ____

6. **Count 6:** Recover right arm through vertical, pull left arm, kick right leg ____

7. **Count 1:** Roll right, place right hand in and stretch, finish left-arm pull, kick left leg ____

**Follow-Through Phase**

1. Continue in rhythm, hips up, head steady ____

# Detecting Errors in Back Crawl Stroke

Common errors in the leg kick and the arm-stroke have been addressed in Steps 3 and 4, respectively. Errors in body position and coordination also occur. Some of them follow with suggestions for correcting them.

| ERROR | CORRECTION |
|---|---|
| 1. Coordination degenerates. | 1. Slow down, start over. |
| 2. You lose beat count. | 2. Count aloud. |
| 3. Hand entry on 1 or 4 is imprecise. | 3. Slap your hand and arm on the water precisely on the count. |
| 4. Water gets in your face from above your head. | 4. Drop your chin a little. |
| 5. Kick becomes horizontal. | 5. Use less hip roll. |
| 6. Feet slide side to side. | 6. Roll your hips more, keep your elbow in close to your side. |

# Back Crawl Stroke Drills

## 1. One-Arm Drill

Start kicking in back glide position with both arms stretched overhead, palms out. Count kicks in 6-beat cycles. On the third count of 1, roll slightly to the right, reach forward, and catch the water by bending your wrist. Pull through on Counts 2 and 3. On 4 press down with your right hand, roll to the left, and lift your right shoulder. Leave your left arm stretched overhead as you recover your right arm on 5 and 6. Roll strongly back to the right side as your right hand strikes the water on the next count of 1. Continue to pull with your right arm only, leaving your left arm stretched overhead.

Repeat the drill, now pulling with your left arm only, leaving your right arm stretched overhead. Make your left hand strike the water on 4, and roll your shoulder up on 1.

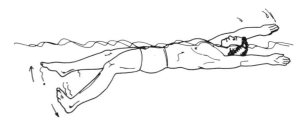

**Success Goal =**

50 yards or meters with each arm

**Your Score =**

(#) _____ yards or meters with each arm

## 2. Slow-Motion Drill

Wear a float belt near your hips for this drill, if it appears to help. Swim the back crawl stroke very slowly, counting the kicks at about one per second. Swim using both arms but concentrate on the full cycle of one arm for several strokes, then shift your concentration to the other arm for a few strokes. Finally, concentrate on the coordination between arms and legs for a few strokes. Keep the pace very slow. Avoid the tendency to speed up.

**Success Goal** = 100 yards or meters of continuous slow-motion swimming

**Your Score** = (#) _____ yards or meters of slow-motion swimming

## 3. Normal Back Crawl Stroke

Always be alert to judge your distance from the end of the pool. Use lane float color changes or backstroke turn flags to prevent injury. If your pool does not have turn flags or lane floats, place chairs or other markers at the sides of the pool, 15 feet from each end of the pool.

Swim an easy, relaxed back crawl stroke at a speed you estimate to be about half as fast as you can swim. Keeping it smooth and rhythmical, swim continuously (except for turns) for 100 yards or meters. Concentrate alternately on each arm, on your kick, and on the coordination of the stroke as you swim.

**Success Goal** = 5 swims of 100 yards or meters each, resting 30 seconds between swims

**Your Score** = (#) _____ swims of 100 yards or meters

# Back Crawl Stroke
# Keys to Success Checklist

Distance alone will not make you a good back crawl stroke swimmer, though it will help. You need someone to watch your stroke and to judge it on a qualitative basis. Ask your coach or teacher to use the checklist within Figure 5.1 to evaluate your stroke.

# *Step 6* **Backstroke Turns**

There are two turns to use while swimming backstroke: the open turn and the tumble turn. You may use the open turn for either the elementary backstroke (see *Swimming: Steps to Success*, Step 16) or the back crawl stroke. It will be described here as used with the back crawl stroke. The open turn is so named because your head remains above water, allowing you to take a breath during the turn. It is not used in competitive swimming.

The tumble turn is a closed turn, that is, your head remains underwater during the turn with no opportunity to breathe. It is the turn that competitive swimmers use in backstroke races and is designed solely for high speed.

## WHY ARE THE BACKSTROKE TURNS IMPORTANT?

It is easy to misjudge your distance from the end of the pool when swimming on your back. Dangerous head injuries could result from failure to execute a turn properly. It is important, therefore, that you be able to use a simple, safe, and easy method for changing direction while swimming in a pool.

The open backstroke turn is the easiest of the backstroke turns and will be used at earlier stages in learning the backstroke than will the tumble turn, its competitive swimming counterpart. In addition, you may use the open turn for any stroke on the back, whereas you may use the tumble turn only with the back crawl stroke. Yet, the backstroke tumble turn is very important to competitive swimmers and is essential for the repertoire of anyone who wishes to be an advanced or skilled swimmer.

## HOW TO DO THE OPEN BACKSTROKE TURN

To help judge your distance, use backstroke turn flags, colored lane line floats, or a marker you have placed at the side of the pool 15 feet from the end of the pool. Swim the back crawl stroke toward the end of the pool. When your head passes the flags, colored floats, or marker, finish the pull in progress and take two more.

As you finish the second pull, roll completely onto your side on the outstretched forward arm, streamline your body, and glide into the wall. As your hand touches the wall, grasp the edge of the pool and pull, tuck your knees quickly, and bring both feet under you as you turn to face the wall. Take a big breath, release the wall as you float through the pivot, lay your head back and place both feet against the wall just under the surface, place both hands by your ears palm up, and push off just under the surface. Extend your arms as you push off, streamline your body, and exhale slowly through your nose as you glide under the surface. When your speed slows to swimming speed, kick to the surface and resume swimming the back crawl (see Figure 6.1).

If your pool has a flat wall with no place to grasp, glide in, place your palm flat against the wall, allow your elbow to bend until your head is near the wall, then press downward with your hand to initiate the pivot in a tuck position. Try to stay as close to the wall as possible to ensure a good push-off.

## HOW TO DO THE BACKSTROKE TUMBLE TURN

Rule books governing competitive backstroke races are quite specific as to markings and warnings to be used for backstroke competition. All rule books specify using backstroke warning flags suspended over the pool 15 feet (National Collegiate Athletic Association) or 5 meters (U.S. Swimming, long course) from the end of the pool. They also require using lane float lines that have a distinctive color marking the same distances. Consult current rule books for exact specifications. Because the tumble turn is used only for competition, we will assume that the pool you are using is so equipped.

Experiment carefully to determine exactly how many full-speed backstroke arm pulls you need between the time your head passes under the backstroke warning flags and the point from which you can glide strongly into the wall with your forward arm outstretched. Count your strokes carefully; when you have completed your last pull, stay flat on your back and stretch your forward arm overhead and deep so it will contact the wall directly in front of your head, about 12 inches under the surface, with the fingertips pointed downward and inward. Continue to kick strongly but be ready to react instantly when your forward hand touches the wall. Inhale deeply as you stretch and kick.

As your forward hand touches the wall, absorb the shock by allowing your elbow to bend until it almost touches the wall. At the same time, turn your other hand palm up at your hip and pull strongly with your abdominal muscles to tuck and lift your legs out of the water. Your head will submerge at this point, and you must begin a long exhalation that will continue until you emerge from your push-off and glide. Push up and away from the wall with your forward hand and scoop strongly out and around toward your head with your other hand. This will cause a rotation of your body as if you were spinning on your back on the surface of the water, exactly like break-dancers used to spin on the sidewalks of New York. If you touch with your right hand, your feet should spin to the right while your left hand scoops out and presses upward toward your head to hasten the spin.

Continue to scoop with one hand and push the water toward your hips with the other until the scooping hand is just above your head and your other hand is about to touch your hip. By that time your feet should be pointing toward the wall. Drop your feet from above the water to a depth of about 18 inches and begin to extend your knees to plant the balls of your feet solidly against the wall. Leave your scooping hand at ear level, palm up; bring your other hand underwater from your hip to your other ear, palm up. Continue to exhale through your nose; push strongly with both feet as you extend your arms overhead, drop your head back, and lift your hips into a streamlined position for an underwater glide. Glide until you slow to swimming speed, then kick to the surface and resume stroking (see Figure 6.1).

## Figure 6.1 Keys to Success: Backstroke Turns

**Preparation Phase**

| Open Turn | Tumble Turn |
|---|---|
| 1. Judge distance from wall, ____ select proper hand | ____ |

# Execution
# Phase

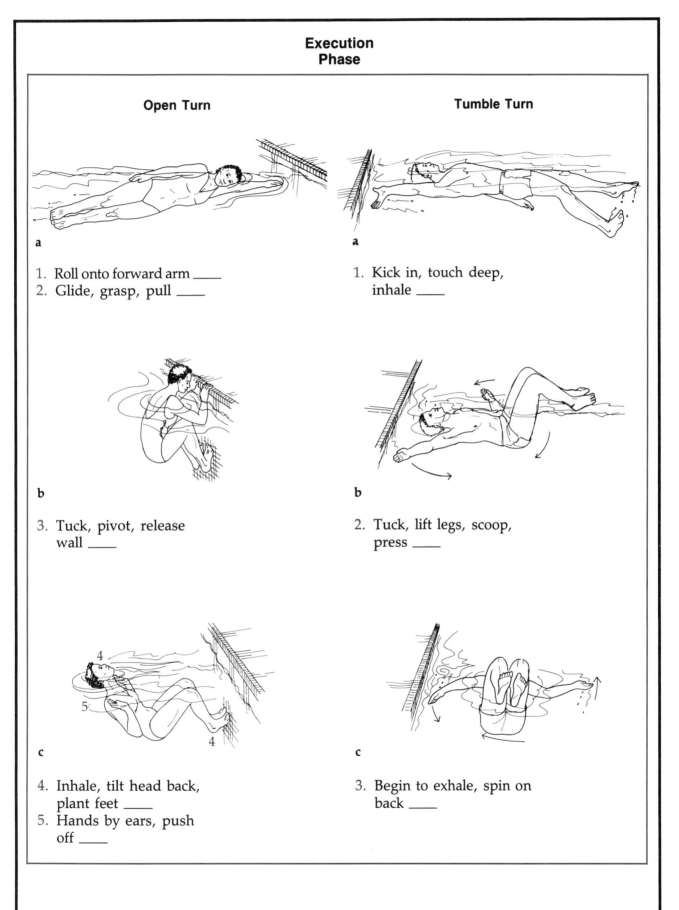

**Open Turn**

a

1. Roll onto forward arm ____
2. Glide, grasp, pull ____

b

3. Tuck, pivot, release wall ____

c

4. Inhale, tilt head back, plant feet ____
5. Hands by ears, push off ____

**Tumble Turn**

a

1. Kick in, touch deep, inhale ____

b

2. Tuck, lift legs, scoop, press ____

c

3. Begin to exhale, spin on back ____

### Open Turn

### Tumble Turn

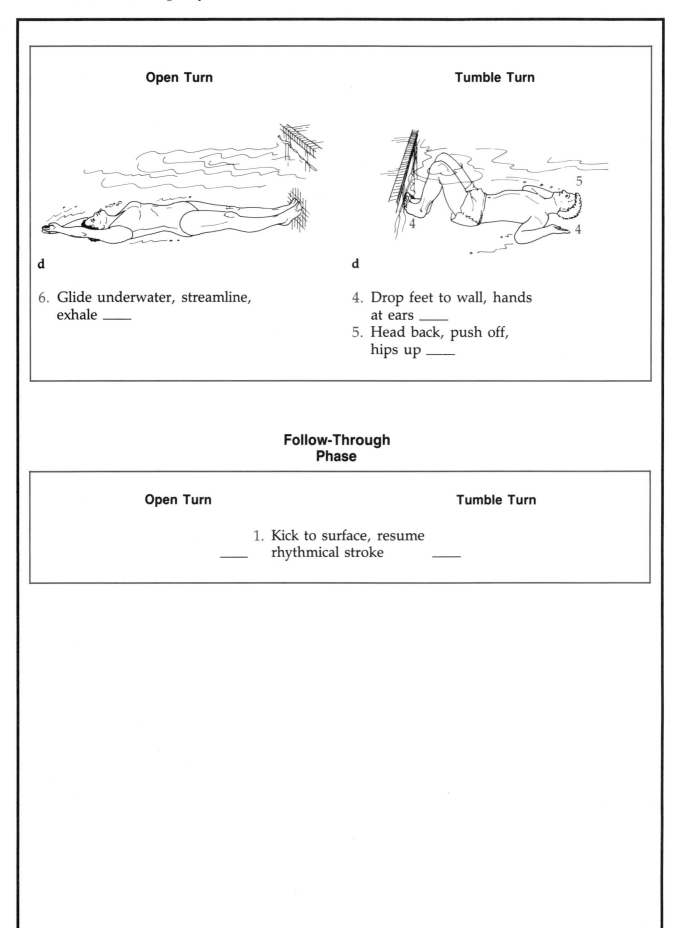

d

d

6. Glide underwater, streamline, exhale ____

4. Drop feet to wall, hands at ears ____
5. Head back, push off, hips up ____

### Follow-Through
### Phase

**Open Turn**

**Tumble Turn**

____  1. Kick to surface, resume rhythmical stroke  ____

# Detecting Errors in the Backstroke Turns

Backstroke turns are complex maneuvers with many things happening at once. There are several common errors you may understandably make while learning these turns. They follow with suggestions for correcting them.

**ERROR** ⊘

**CORRECTION**

## Open Backstroke Turn

1. You roll too far before touch.

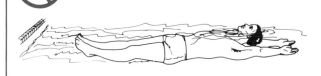

2. You pivot too slowly.
3. You push off on surface.

4. Nose gets full of water.

5. You surface too quickly.

6. You hold glide too long.
7. You get stuck underwater.

1. Keep upper arm back slightly.

2. Tuck more tightly.
3. Sink under before pushing, head back, hips up.

4. Exhale more steadily throughout underwater glide.

5. Keep head back, arms back, hips up.

6. Begin kick before surfacing.
7. Use first armstroke to rise.

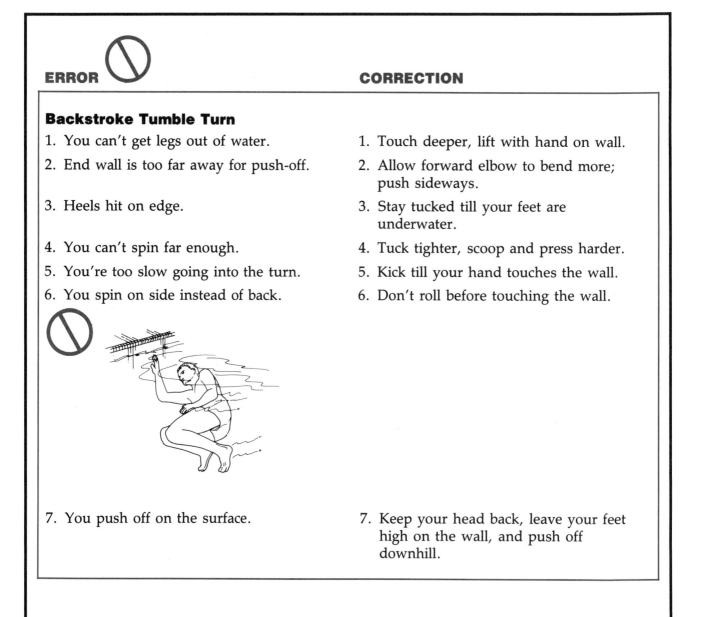

**ERROR**                                                   **CORRECTION**

**Backstroke Tumble Turn**

| ERROR | CORRECTION |
|---|---|
| 1. You can't get legs out of water. | 1. Touch deeper, lift with hand on wall. |
| 2. End wall is too far away for push-off. | 2. Allow forward elbow to bend more; push sideways. |
| 3. Heels hit on edge. | 3. Stay tucked till your feet are underwater. |
| 4. You can't spin far enough. | 4. Tuck tighter, scoop and press harder. |
| 5. You're too slow going into the turn. | 5. Kick till your hand touches the wall. |
| 6. You spin on side instead of back. | 6. Don't roll before touching the wall. |
| 7. You push off on the surface. | 7. Keep your head back, leave your feet high on the wall, and push off downhill. |

# Open Backstroke Turn Drills

## 1. Open Backstroke Turn Push-Off With Nose Clip

Position a nose clip on your nose carefully. It should be relatively comfortable and should block your nose completely. Goggles are optional, but you may have trouble keeping them in place.

From a prone position in the water, facing the end wall, grasp the edge of the pool overflow trough with both hands. (Note: You may grasp the pool coping if it is not more than 4 inches above the water surface. If no handhold is within 4 inches of the water, place both palms flat against the wall at water level and keep them there by kicking in the prone position.) Pull with both hands as you tuck your legs and bring them through under your body to place both feet against the wall, the toes about 4 inches beneath the surface. (Note: With no handhold, press downward with both hands to bring your tightly tucked legs under you and into the wall.) Lay your head back until your face is about 3 inches under the water, then stay tucked as you bring both hands quickly underwater to a palm-up position by your ears.

Push with your legs and extend your arms overhead as you bring your hips up into a streamlined glide position just under the water. Use your arm and head position to stay submerged for a 3-second glide. Then begin the back crawl kick to the surface and pull through with one arm to start the back crawl stroke.

**Success Goal** = 10 push-offs in good position, with controlled underwater glide

**Your Score** = (#) _____ push-offs in good position, with controlled underwater glide

## 2. Open Backstroke Turn Push-Off With Mouth Breathing

Repeat Drill 1 but begin exhaling through your mouth as your head sinks under before the push-off. Continue your exhalation steadily throughout the underwater glide. Some practice in breath control will be necessary to maintain a steady stream of bubbles until you reach the surface at the end of your glide. It is very important that you learn this breath control skill before moving to the next drill. Using your voice as you exhale often helps maintain a steady bubble rate.

**Success Goal** = 10 consecutive push-offs with steady stream of bubbles while underwater

**Your Score** = (#) _____ consecutive steady-bubble push-offs

## 3. Breath Control for the Open Backstroke Turn

This will be the most difficult drill for the open backstroke turn, but the breath control skill will also be necessary for the competitive (closed) backstroke tumble turn. Improper technique here would result in water entering your nose, causing considerable distress, so practice Drill 2 until you can exhale steadily for the entire time your face is underwater.

Then remove your nose clip and repeat Drill 2, except that you must exhale steadily through your *nose*. Keep your mouth closed tightly. Do not be discouraged by the first few tries; you can do it with a little practice.

**Success Goal** = 10 consecutive back push-offs in good form without getting water in your nose

**Your Score** = (#) _____ consecutive back push-offs in good form without getting water in your nose

## 4. *Side Glide Into Backstroke Open Turn*

Goggles are optional. Do the drill without a nose clip, if possible. Start about 15 feet from the end of the pool in a back glide position, arms overhead. Take three back crawl pulls, starting with your left arm. As your left arm pulls through the third stroke, roll onto your right side, look at the end wall, and glide with your right arm extended and your left hand resting on your thigh. Do not roll past the vertical onto your stomach.

As your right hand reaches the end wall, grasp the gutter, pull, tuck, and roll to face the wall as your feet come through under you. Do not bring your left hand to the wall, but place it immediately beside your ear, palm up. Release your right handhold, place your right hand beside your right ear, and push off as in Drill 3.

(If no handhold is available on the end wall, place your right palm flat against the end wall, allow your elbow to bend to get you in close, and press downward with your hand to initiate a pivot in the tucked position. As your feet come through under you, press backward on the water as you bring your right hand up to your ear. This backward press of the right hand will push you into the wall.)

Repeat the drill but start pulling with your right arm so you will glide into the wall on your left side.

**Success Goal** = 5 smooth-flowing turns on each side

**Your Score** = (#) _____ smooth-flowing turns on each side

## 5. *Open Backstroke Turn*

Wear a nose clip only if you have been unsuccessful in controlling your breathing properly in Drills 3 and 4. Goggles are optional. Place a marker of some kind 15 feet or 5 meters from the end of the pool; use backstroke turn flags if they are available. You may also use competitive lane float markers that are of a contrasting color for the last 15 feet or 5 meters before they attach to the wall. If neither flags nor lane lines are available, place a chair or another marker at the pool's side edge at the proper distance from the end wall.

Start from a point about 40 feet from the end of the pool. Swim back crawl toward the end of the pool until your head is even with the marker. Complete the pull then in progress and take two more armstrokes. As you complete the second pull, roll onto your forward arm and leave your trailing hand resting on your thigh. Glide into the wall in side glide position. As your forward arm reaches the wall, perform the turn and push-off exactly as you did in Drill 4.

After practicing a few times, you may find that when your head passes the marker, you need to take three strokes instead of two to avoid gliding too long. Be very careful in determining the correct number of strokes so you don't strike the wall with your head. Also, vary your strokes during the drill so that you get practice in turning to either side.

**Success Goal** = 10 smooth and efficient turns on each side

**Your Score** = (#) _____ smooth and efficient turns on each side

# Backstroke Tumble Turn Drills

## 1. *Choosing Which Arm to Use*

Begin about 25 feet from the end of the pool. Swim back crawl toward the end at nearly full speed. As your head passes under the turn flag line, finish the arm pull in progress, take two more strokes, and hold with one arm extended overhead and the other along your side.

Continue to kick, though, and count your kicks from the moment you stop stroking until your forward hand touches the wall. If you count more than six kicks before your hand touches, start again and add one more stroke after passing the flag line. Keep trying until you discover how many armstrokes you must take to touch the wall in less than six kicks. Deliberately change the arm with which you pass the turn flags so you will touch with each hand. Practice until you can *consistently* judge the point at which to stop stroking to touch the wall within six kicks. Make all trials near top speed.

**Success Goal** = 10 consecutive trials in which you touch the wall within 6 kicks after stopping your armstroke, making some touches with each hand

**Your Score** = (#) _____ consecutive successful trials, including some with each hand

## 2. *Backstroke Tumble Turn Land Drill*

Place a foam plastic tumbling mat on the pool deck with the end against a wall. The mat should be at least 6 feet long. Wet the mat and your back. Lie on your back on the mat, with your head toward the wall, right arm overhead with your palm flat against the wall, elbow slightly bent, and your left arm by your side.

Suddenly tuck and lift your legs, rolling up nearly onto your shoulder blades. Push sideways against the wall with your right hand and push outward from your body with your left hand, initiating a spinning motion of your body. Your feet should spin to the right in tuck position. Your left hand should push outward until it is above your head; leave it there. Your right hand should sweep out sideways until it comes to your side; bring it immediately to your right ear. When your feet are at the wall, push gently with them to full extension. Extend both arms overhead as you push. Be careful not to slide off the mat.

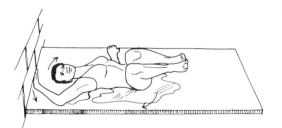

Repeat the drill with your left hand overhead and your right arm down, spinning to the left. Note that you initiate the tuck with your stomach muscles but you initiate the spin with your arms. Your feet always turn toward your touching hand.

**Success Goal =**

10 smooth turns in each direction

**Your Score =**

(#) ____ smooth turns in each direction

## 3. Back Spin, Floating

Wear a nose clip for this drill. Goggles are optional. Assume a back floating position away from any pool wall. Scull your body up into a horizontal position, then, before your feet sink, extend your right arm overhead and your left arm down along your side. Tuck both knees while floating, turn your left palm up, and press outward with both arms simultaneously in a wide, sweeping motion that spins your feet to the right. Try to spin in your back floating tuck position until you are headed in the opposite direction, then extend your legs again.

Practice until you can make the turn exactly 180 degrees with one continuous sweeping motion. Reverse the arm positions and try the drill spinning to the left.

**Success Goal =**

10 180-degree spins in each direction

**Your Score =**

(#) ____ 180-degree spins in each direction

## 4. Backstroke Tumble Turns in Midpool

Wear a nose clip while practicing this drill. Goggles are optional. Swim back crawl stroke away from any pool edge. Stop stroking suddenly with your right arm overhead and your left arm at your side. Reach deep into the water directly overhead with your right hand palm up, and drop your head back to look directly at your right hand. Lifting upward and outward with your right hand, lift and tuck your legs up above the water. As your feet lift, continue the outward sweep toward your hip with your right hand and sweep your left arm out from your side, palm up, toward your head. Spin your body so your feet move over the water to the right, toward your right hand. In effect, you feel as though you are throwing your legs over your right shoulder. When your body has turned exactly 180 degrees, extend your legs as they drop back into the water. You should now be headed in the opposite direction.

Practice the turn until you can spin exactly 180 degrees. Then reverse the arm positions and spin to the left until you can turn quickly and fluently.

**Success Goal** = 10 midpool tumble turns in each direction

**Your Score** = (#) _____ quick, fluid tumble turns in each direction

## 5. Backstroke Tumble Turn With Nose Clip

Wear a nose clip for this drill. Goggles are optional. Start swimming back crawl stroke at about midpool. As you pass under the backstroke turn flags, count your strokes to judge your hand-touch properly. Continue kicking and reach deep to touch the wall.

As your hand touches, tuck and lift your legs out of the water; meanwhile, sweep wide with both arms and spin on your back and shoulders to "throw" your feet over the shoulder of the touching hand. *CAUTION: To avoid hitting your heels on the wall, stay tucked tightly until your feet drop into the water.* As your feet drop under, place your hands palm up by each ear, push against the wall with the balls of your feet, extend your arms overhead, and streamline your body for an underwater glide. As you slow down to swimming speed, kick to the surface and resume stroking.

**Success Goal** = 10 correct turns to each side

**Your Score** = (#) _____ correct turns to each side

## 6. *Backstroke Tumble Turns Without Nose Clip*

Start this drill with a nose clip. Goggles are optional. Repeat Drill 5 but begin a slow, steady exhalation through your mouth as soon as your head submerges after the hand-touch. Continue to exhale throughout the turn and push-off and until you surface after your glide.

Use your nose clip as you learn to control your breathing through your mouth, until you can consistently maintain a steady exhalation for the entire time required. After you master the breath control with the nose clip, try the turn without your nose clip and exhale through your nose instead of your mouth. Keep your lips tightly closed. Using your voice to ''hum out'' the air often helps the transition.

**Success Goal** = 10 consecutive turns without a nose clip and without getting water in your nose

**Your Score** = (#) _____ consecutive successful turns without a nose clip

## 7. *Backstroke Tumble Turns, Timed*

Have a friend use a stopwatch or timer to time your turns. Your friend starts the timer when your head passes under the backstroke turn flags as you swim back crawl stroke into a turn. He or she stops the timer when your head again passes under the flags on the way out of the turn.

When you can do the turn smoothly in 10 seconds, you are becoming proficient. If you can do it in 8 seconds, you have achieved skilled swimmer status. A time under 8 seconds puts you into the competitive swimmer class.

**Success Goal** = 5 out of 10 turns under 10 seconds

**Your Score** = _____ proficient (5 out of 10 under 10 seconds)
_____ skilled (8 out of 10 under 8 seconds)
_____ competitive (10 consecutive turns under 8 seconds)

# Backstroke Turns
# Keys to Success Checklist

Practice makes perfect only if you are practicing the correct procedures. Repetition alone is not enough to ensure perfection. You need to have a coach or a teacher evaluate your techniques from a qualitative standpoint to determine whether you have been practicing the skills properly. Use the checklist within Figure 6.1.

## *Step 7* **Dolphin Kick**

The dolphin kick is humankind's attempt to emulate the powerful swimming motions of the creatures of the sea. The gentle, sleek, smiling bottlenose dolphin was one model selected for imitation in our search for more efficient modes of locomotion in the aquatic medium. It is sometimes called the "fishtail" kick, but its vertical plane of motion more nearly resembles that of sea mammals.

### WHY IS THE DOLPHIN KICK IMPORTANT?

The dolphin kick is quite powerful and great fun. It has considerable versatility in its application and is an important step in attaining true watermanship. To date, however, its greatest importance has been in its use for competitive swimming. It can be used in several strokes but has been used primarily in the butterfly. It is described here as the first step in learning that stroke. Later in this text, we will explore its use in other situations.

### HOW TO DO THE DOLPHIN KICK

We must think of the dolphin kick not so much as a leg kick, but as an undulation of the whole body culminating in a whipping motion of the feet. Keep the picture of a dolphin in mind all the time you do this kick.

Begin the kick in a prone floating position with both arms stretched in front of you. Hold your breath and keep your face in the water as you do this kick. Think of your body as being a perfectly flexible rubber cylinder floating on the waves. As an imaginary wave approaches, flex your wrists to guide your hands up, over, and down the other side of the wave. Your arms, shoulders, chest, waist, hips, and knees flex in turn to follow the passage of the wave under you. As your legs are passing over the top of the wave, your hands are already turning upward to ride over the next wave. As the wave passes under you, your body curls slightly forward and then arches into the trough as your legs rise behind you. Leave your ankles perfectly relaxed as you lift your legs and as your hips drop. As the crest of the wave passes your feet, press it downward and backward with the tops of your feet, ankles extended.

Continue to undulate, but direct your attention to your legs. As your legs move downward, allow your knees to bend. The downward motion will cause your floppy ankles to extend and your toes to point. Forcibly straighten your knees and flip the water downward and backward with your floppy feet. As your legs start up, allow your knees to straighten.

Continue the rhythmic undulation of your body, alternately lifting and pressing with floppy ankles. Keep your legs close together and move them simultaneously in a vertical plane. Emphasize the downward thrust and flipping action of the lower legs and feet (see Figure 7.1).

*Figure 7.1 Keys to Success:*
*Dolphin Kick*

**Preparation Phase**

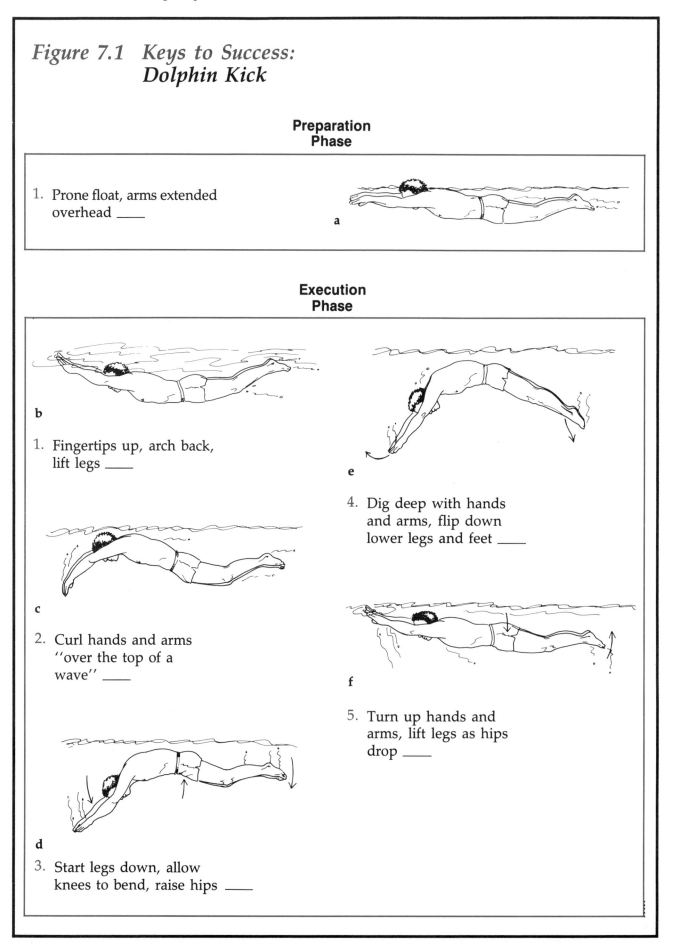

1. Prone float, arms extended overhead ____

a

**Execution Phase**

b

1. Fingertips up, arch back, lift legs ____

c

2. Curl hands and arms "over the top of a wave" ____

d

3. Start legs down, allow knees to bend, raise hips ____

e

4. Dig deep with hands and arms, flip down lower legs and feet ____

f

5. Turn up hands and arms, lift legs as hips drop ____

**Follow-Through
Phase**

1. Continue rhythmic
   undulation ____

# Detecting Errors in the Dolphin Kick

Several common errors are evident as swimmers learn the dolphin kick. Some of them are listed here. A suggestion for corrective action is listed with each error.

**ERROR**

**CORRECTION**

1. Only lower legs kick.
2. Only hips bend.
3. Toes stay rigidly pointed.
4. You bend too deeply at hips.

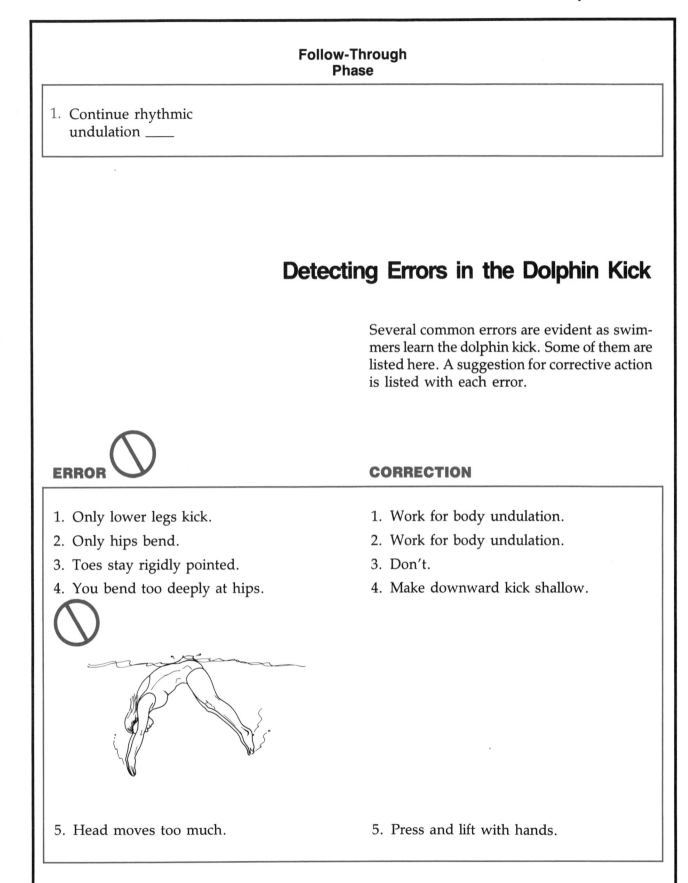

5. Head moves too much.

1. Work for body undulation.
2. Work for body undulation.
3. Don't.
4. Make downward kick shallow.

5. Press and lift with hands.

# Dolphin Kick Drills

## 1. Sideways Fishtail

Goggles are recommended. At the end of the pool, take a breath and submerge on your side. Push off from the wall underwater on your side, arms stretched overhead. Remain on your side with feet together as you begin an undulating body motion culminating in a lower-leg kick (a) and a flip of your relaxed feet (b). Pretend you are a fish; imitate the way you think a fish moves.

Start fairly deep and try to stay underwater as you kick. Go as far as you can on one breath before surfacing. Remember to kick both forward and backward with your feet.

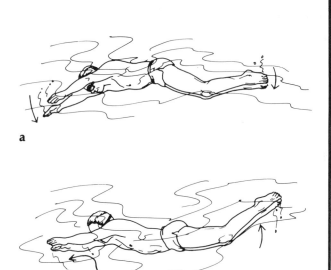

**Success Goal =**

30 feet fishtailing underwater

**Your Score =**

(#) ____ feet fishtailing underwater

## 2. Fishtail Kick With Fins

Don socks or boots and swim fins. Wear goggles. Repeat Drill 1 with fins. Keep both arms overhead for safety. You will move so fast that you may run into a wall before you realize it.

**Success Goal =** 60 feet underwater on one breath

**Your Score =** (#) ____ feet underwater on one breath

## 3. Fishtail, Roll to Dolphin Kick

Repeat Drill 2, but after starting on your side (a), continue to kick as you roll into a face-down position (b). Try to stay underwater as you finish the distance in prone position (c). Then do the drill again, starting in the prone position and remaining on your stomach throughout.

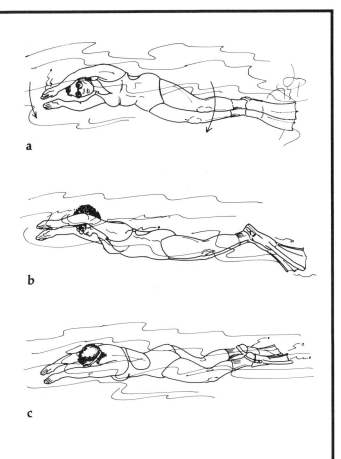

**Success Goal =**

60 feet of underwater dolphin kick on one breath

**Your Score =**

(#) _____ feet of dolphin kick

## 4. Dolphin Kick With Kickboard

Goggles are optional. Don socks or boots and swim fins. Hold a kickboard at arm's length in front of you. Keep your arms stretched up in front of you as you push off from the wall on your stomach. Begin a small undulation from your hips, culminating in a small downward flip of both fins. Do not emphasize the upward lift of your fins but allow them to rise as the result of your hips' dropping while your body undulates. Keep your ankles completely relaxed. Continue to flip your fins repeatedly downward against the water. Try to keep the fins underwater by pressing on the kickboard. Exhale with your face in the water and thrust your chin forward to the surface to inhale. Exhale during two kicks, inhale during one. Kick slowly and easily.

**Success Goal** = ability to kick slowly for 100 yards or meters without undue fatigue

**Your Score** = (#) _____ yards or meters dolphin kick with ease

## 5. Underwater Dolphin Kick, No Fins

Goggles are recommended. Push off in prone position underwater from the end of the pool. Flex your wrists to turn your fingertips upward as you arch your back and bend your knees slightly, raising your heels and preparing to start your kick. Remain underwater as you start to kick downward and backward with floppy ankles. Guide your hands upward, over an "underwater wave," then downward to dig deeply into the water ahead. As you kick downward, the rest of your body should follow the path of your hands, undulating up and over the imaginary wave and sliding down the other side. Dig your hands into the water and lift with the backs of your hands against the water as you raise your heels again for a second kick.

**Success Goal =** kick for 30 feet underwater

**Your Score =** (#) _____ feet of underwater dolphin kick

## 6. Variation on the Underwater Kick

Repeat Drill 5 but leave your arms relaxed at your sides as you kick underwater. Wear goggles so you can see where you are going. Be careful not to kick into the wall. Some people find it much easier to kick with their arms down.

**Success Goal =**

30 feet of underwater kick with arms down

**Your Score**

(#) _____ feet underwater with arms down

## 7. Dolphin Kick With Kickboard, No Fins

Wear goggles and hold a kickboard with both hands. Do a dolphin kick on the surface. Leave your face in the water while you exhale for two or more kicks; press on the kickboard to help you raise your head when you want a breath. Kick mostly with your legs from the knees down. Bend your knees as you drop them under, then flip your relaxed feet downward and backward against the water. Keep the kick small, and kick slowly. Feel the undulation in your torso as your hips move up and down.

**Success Goal =** 50 yards or meters of slow dolphin kick

**Your Score =** (#) _____ yards or meters of easy dolphin kick

## 8. Paired Dolphin Kicks

Use goggles and a kickboard. Prepare to do a small dolphin kick with your face in the water. Do two downward kicks in rapid succession, then stop. Slowly raise your feet in preparation for the next kick. Kick downward again twice in rapid succession, then stop again while you raise your legs slowly. Exhale during the two kicks; raise your chin to breathe during the stop period.

Start to count while you kick. As your legs kick downward, count "one." As your legs lift, count "and." On the second downward kick, count "two." During the stop count a very slow and drawn-out "a-a-n-d" as you raise your legs for the next pair of kicks. Thus, for two rapid kicks and a stop, the count is "one, and, two, a-a-n-d." Continue to kick and count with paired kicks.

**Success Goal** = 50 yards or meters using paired kicks and counting

**Your Score** = (#) _____ yards or meters with paired kicks in steady stop-beat rhythm

# Dolphin Kick
# Keys to Success Checklist

Distance alone does not indicate the degree of skill with which you execute the dolphin kick. You need the opinion of an expert to tell you whether all your body parts are functioning smoothly in the flow pattern for the kick. Have an expert use the checklist within Figure 7.1 to give you a quality rating on your kick.

# Step 8  Butterfly Stroke Arm Pull

The butterfly stroke is often said to be the most difficult of the swimming strokes because both arms recover over the water simultaneously. For some who have exceptionally tight shoulder joints, it may prove to be bothersome, but most swimmers can learn to do it with an easy, relaxed motion. It cannot be hurried; it must be long and full, with a relaxed recovery.

## WHY IS THE BUTTERFLY ARM PULL IMPORTANT?

The butterfly stroke arm pull is a major component of an important competitive swimming stroke. As such, it is a step in the learning progression for the stroke. Also, it is the only swimming stroke performed in the prone position in which the arms recover simultaneously over the water.

## HOW TO DO THE BUTTERFLY STROKE ARM PULL

The propulsive portions of this stroke and the crawl stroke are nearly identical. Review the crawl stroke arm pull in Step 1. Both strokes start in a prone float position with both arms extended overhead in line with your shoulders. To do the butterfly armstroke, pull with both arms simultaneously. Flex both wrists to point your fingertips downward and, by bending your elbows slightly, turn your palms slightly outward. Begin the pull by slicing (sculling) your hands outward, around, and inward, bending your elbows and turning your palms to facilitate the sculling action as if you were trying to draw a large circle with your fingertips on the bottom of the pool. Leave your elbows as far forward as you can during the first half of the circle, pulling with your hands and forearms. Bring your shoulder

muscles into play by beginning to pull with your upper arms as your hands and forearms pass your ears. With elbows bent at 90 degrees, press back and inward toward the centerline of your body until your hands complete the circle, nearly touching under your chest. Allow your wrists to begin bending back to keep the palms perpendicular to the line of effort (they will be forced into that position if you simply relax them slowly as you push). Push straight backward toward your feet, extending your elbows and separating your hands enough for them to pass, palms up, outside your thighs.

Keep your elbows straight as you lift both arms free of the water. Begin to bring both arms forward over the water with palms facing upward until your arms are nearly at shoulder level. At that point begin to turn your palms down and continue to bring both arms over the water to enter as far forward as you can reach, in line with your shoulders. Keep your elbows high on the entry, as though you were reaching over a wave with both arms. Allow your head, hands, and upper torso to dive "over a wave" to about a foot beneath the water, then bend your wrists back to turn the fingertips up and glide toward the surface. As soon as your hands return to the surface, flex your wrists to drop your fingertips in preparation for the next stroke. Do not begin the next stroke as your hands enter the water. Allow time to dive, reach, and glide to the surface before starting the next stroke.

The whole stroke resembles drawing a keyhole with your hands: The circle at the top followed by a straight push from your chest to your thighs circumscribes a keyhole shape. Simply do a crawl stroke with both arms simultaneously (see Figure 8.1).

*Figure 8.1  Keys to Success:*
**Butterfly Stroke**
**Arm Pull**

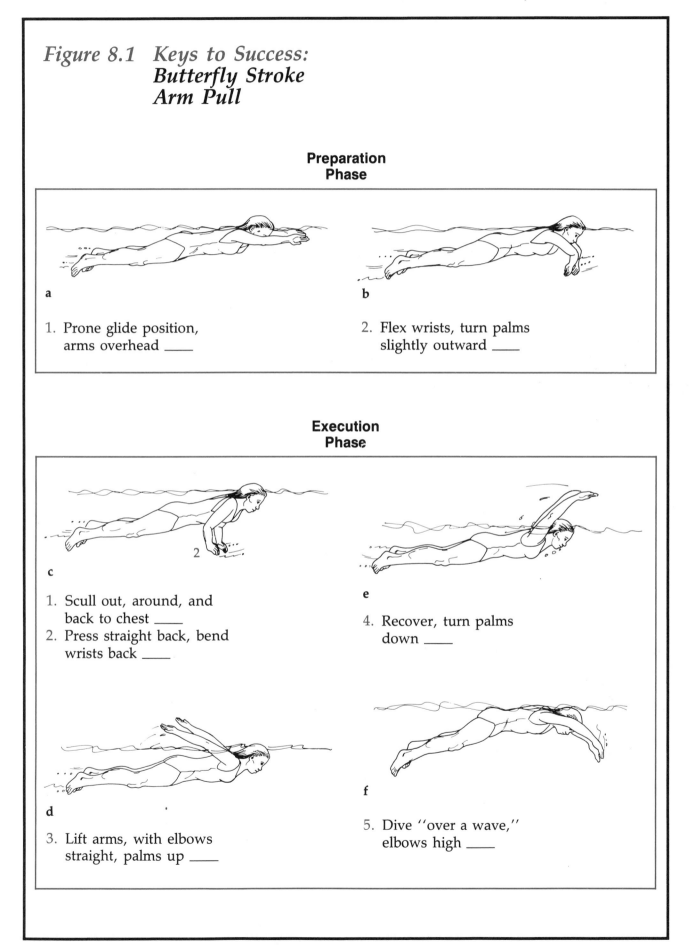

**Preparation**
**Phase**

a

1. Prone glide position,
   arms overhead ___

b

2. Flex wrists, turn palms
   slightly outward ___

**Execution**
**Phase**

c

1. Scull out, around, and
   back to chest ___
2. Press straight back, bend
   wrists back ___

e

4. Recover, turn palms
   down ___

d

3. Lift arms, with elbows
   straight, palms up ___

f

5. Dive ''over a wave,''
   elbows high ___

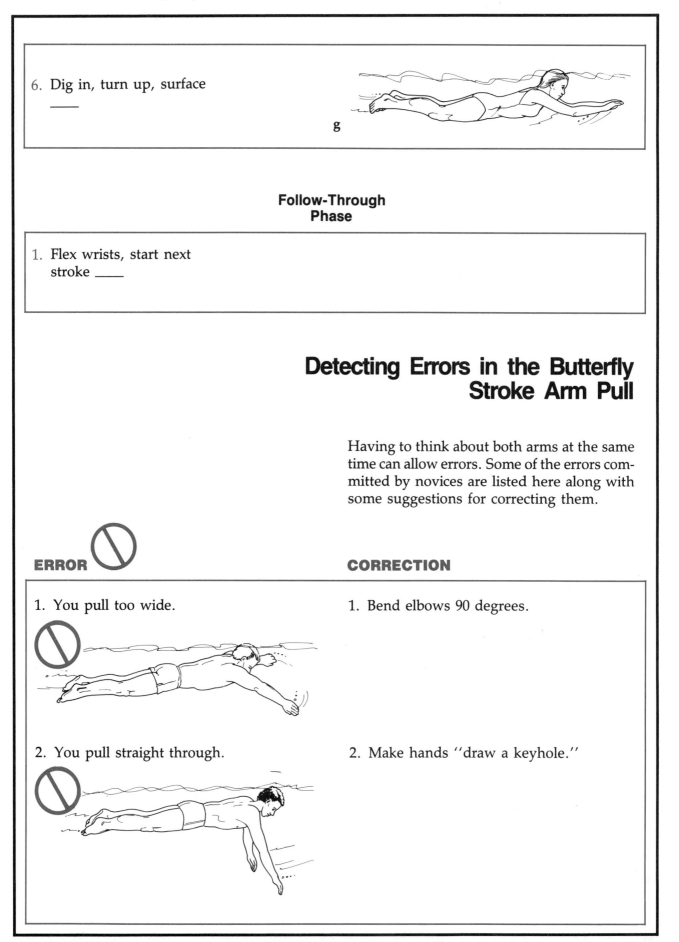

6. Dig in, turn up, surface
——

g

**Follow-Through
Phase**

1. Flex wrists, start next stroke ____

# Detecting Errors in the Butterfly Stroke Arm Pull

Having to think about both arms at the same time can allow errors. Some of the errors committed by novices are listed here along with some suggestions for correcting them.

**ERROR** ⊘

**CORRECTION**

1. You pull too wide.

1. Bend elbows 90 degrees.

2. You pull straight through.

2. Make hands "draw a keyhole."

| ERROR ⊘ | CORRECTION |
|---|---|
| 3. Recovery is too low. | 3. Keep palms up; do stretching exercises. |
| 4. Strokes are continuous. | 4. Dive, then glide to surface. |
| 5. Armstroke is short. | 5. Straighten elbows, push past thighs. |

# Butterfly Stroke Arm Pull Drills

## 1. Slow-Motion Drill With Mask, Snorkel, and Buoyancy Aid

Wear a high-buoyancy float belt near your hips, don a mask and a snorkel, and float facedown. Breathe through the snorkel as you move your arms *very* slowly through the motions of the butterfly arm pull. Stop frequently to study each new position critically. Watch your arms and hands through the mask as they move slowly. Outline a keyhole with your hands as they pull-push. You will sink deeper in the water as your arms begin to lift for the arm recovery. Keep them moving slowly, nevertheless, and go through the motions of the recovery with your shoulders and upper arms partly submerged.

Have someone read the how-to section to you as you try to follow the pattern. Study the pictures (Figure 8.1a-g) again and continue to practice in slow motion. Do not try to get propulsion; just float and move through the patterns.

**Success Goal** = 25 *very* slow-motion strokes

**Your Score** = (#) _____ slow-motion strokes

## 2. Hesitation Butterfly Stroke With Equipment

Don a mask, a snorkel, and a high-buoyancy float belt. Float facedown, breathing through your snorkel. Pull through a butterfly arm pull at moderate speed, but stop at the end of the underwater pull with your arms along your sides, palms up. Hold still and glide for a count of 3 (about 2 or 3 seconds). Then quickly bring your arms forward over the water in the butterfly stroke recovery. Stop again and glide as your hands enter the water overhead. Prepare your hands and arms carefully for the next stroke, then pull again and glide with arms at your sides.

Continue to pull, stop, recover, stop. Pull strongly for distance and try to get your arms as high as you can on the recovery (your shoulders and upper arms will still be partially submerged).

**Success Goal =** 50 yards or meters of hesitation butterfly stroke

**Your Score =** (#) _____ yards or meters of hesitation butterfly stroke

# 3. Hesitation Butterfly Stroke With Breathing

Use a leg float between your thighs. Goggles are recommended. Do not use a mask or a snorkel.

Start in a prone float position with arms extended overhead. Prepare to do a butterfly pull, then exhale sharply just before you begin. As you begin to pull, tilt your head back and thrust your chin sharply to the front until it is at water level. Open your mouth and inhale during the pull. Drop your face into the water again, holding your breath while you stop with arms back and during the recovery of the arms. Exhale while you stop before beginning the next stroke.

**Success Goal =** 50 yards or meters in which you get a breath on every butterfly stroke

**Your Score =** (#) _____ yards or meters with a breath on each butterfly stroke

# 4. Full Butterfly Armstroke and Glide

Repeat Drill 3 but pull through and recover your arms with no hesitation in the arms-back position. Stop and glide for a *full 3 seconds* after each complete pull with recovery. Inhale during the pull. Exhale during the glide. Do not shorten the arm pull; *pull all the way through* on each stroke. Rise only enough to thrust your chin forward to the surface of the water.

**Success Goal =** 25 yards or meters using full butterfly pull and recovery, stopping only with arms overhead

**Your Score =** (#) _____ yards or meters using full pull and recovery

# 5. Butterfly Stroke Arm Pull With Counting

This counting pattern will be *extremely* important in Step 9. Use a leg float between your knees. Goggles are recommended.

Start in the prone float position with arms stretched overhead. Start a butterfly stroke arm pull. Count ''one'' at the midpoint of the pull and take a breath. Count ''and'' as your arms recover. Count ''two'' as your hands strike the water at the completion of the recovery. Count a very long ''a-a-n-d'' as you glide, exhale, and get ready for the next stroke.

Thus, the count will be ''one, and, two, a-a-n-d, one, and, two, a-a-n-d.'' The glide should take about 2 seconds, but each other count will mark only 1 second.

**Success Goal** = 4 butterfly pull trials of 25 yards or meters with correct counting rhythm

**Your Score** = (#) _____ 25 yards or meters trials with correct count

# Butterfly Stroke Arm Pull
# Keys to Success Checklist

Much of this arm pull is hard to visualize. Practicing and counting may help you get the correct rhythm, but it takes a coach or instructor to tell you about the form with which you accomplish the skill. Have an expert watch your arm pull and evaluate it according to the checklist within Figure 8.1.

*Step 9* **Coordinating the Butterfly Stroke**

This unique stroke gets its name from the simultaneous over-water recovery of the arms: As water drips from the trailing edge of the hand and arms, the swimmer looks like a butterfly flying over the water. The butterfly stroke has the reputation of being hard to do because those who have not learned it properly try to rise too high and go too fast. It really requires only moderate effort, if done slowly and easily.

### WHY IS BUTTERFLY STROKE COORDINATION IMPORTANT?

The butterfly stroke is faster than any stroke except the crawl. That fact alone should be enough to establish its importance. It is used for competitive swimming and as another skill on the ladder of watermanship. It is not used for lifesaving, nor as a resting stroke, nor for distance swimming, nor for recreation, but it is sometimes used for its showmanship value as part of a synchronized swimming routine.

### HOW TO COORDINATE THE BUTTERFLY STROKE

You have learned the dolphin kick and the butterfly stroke arm pull. Putting these together in the proper sequence and adding the breathing and rhythm constitutes the butterfly stroke. For exact detail in the move-ments of the legs and the arms, refer back to Steps 7 and 8, respectively.

Start the stroke by kicking the dolphin kick slowly, arms stretched overhead. Time the first arm pull to coincide with a downward kick of your legs. Thrust your chin forward and inhale as you pull. Recover your arms over the water while your legs are lifting. Kick downward again as your head, hands, and arms dive into the water. That is the end of one butterfly stroke. Exhale and, as your legs lift into position to kick again, prepare your hands and arms for another pull. Thus, one armstroke, two downward kicks, and a breath constitute one stroke, but you must take time between strokes to prepare for the next.

The coordination is easily mastered once you understand that the arms complete a cycle in 3 counts, whereas the legs take 4 counts per cycle. The leg cycle is down, up, down, up (4 counts), whereas the arm cycle is pull, recover, enter (3 counts). Your arms *must* wait and prepare for the next stroke while your legs finish the last count. This fact is the greatest single cause of consternation among those who are trying to learn the stroke. The pause in the armstroke may be called a ''glide,'' a ''catch,'' a ''rest,'' or a ''lift,'' but it must be there; do not begin to pull again as soon as your arms enter the water (see Figure 9.1).

*Figure 9.1* **Keys to Success:**
**Butterfly Stroke**
**Coordination**

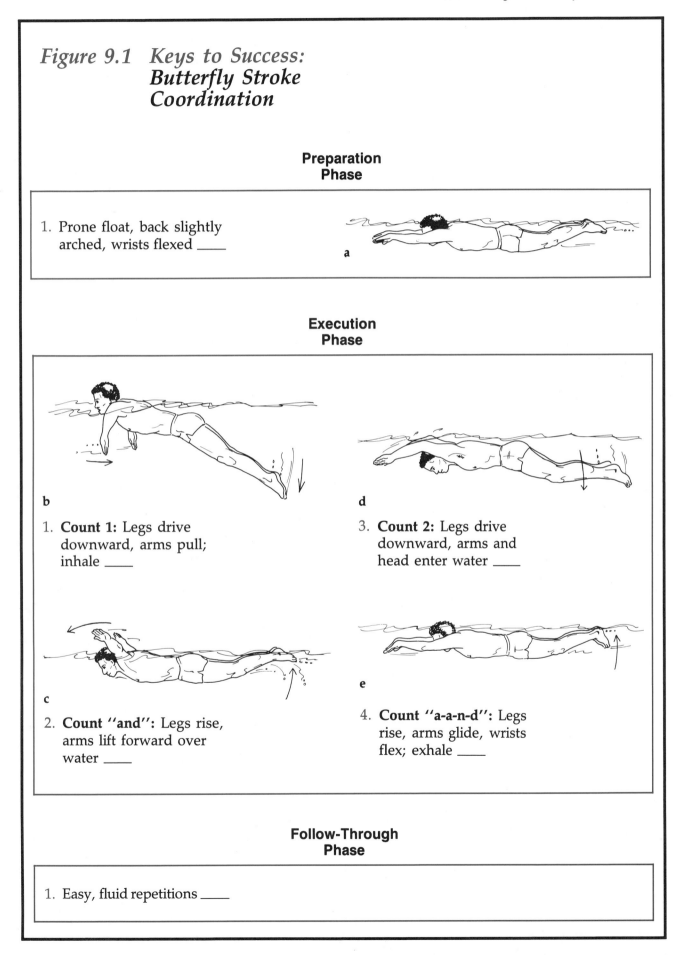

**Preparation**
**Phase**

1. Prone float, back slightly
   arched, wrists flexed ____

a

**Execution**
**Phase**

b

1. **Count 1:** Legs drive
   downward, arms pull;
   inhale ____

d

3. **Count 2:** Legs drive
   downward, arms and
   head enter water ____

c

2. **Count "and":** Legs rise,
   arms lift forward over
   water ____

e

4. **Count "a-a-n-d":** Legs
   rise, arms glide, wrists
   flex; exhale ____

**Follow-Through**
**Phase**

1. Easy, fluid repetitions ____

# Detecting Errors in Butterfly Stroke Coordination

Errors in the kick and the armstroke have been addressed in Steps 7 and 8, respectively. The most common errors in coordination and body position follow with suggestions for their correction.

**ERROR**

**CORRECTION**

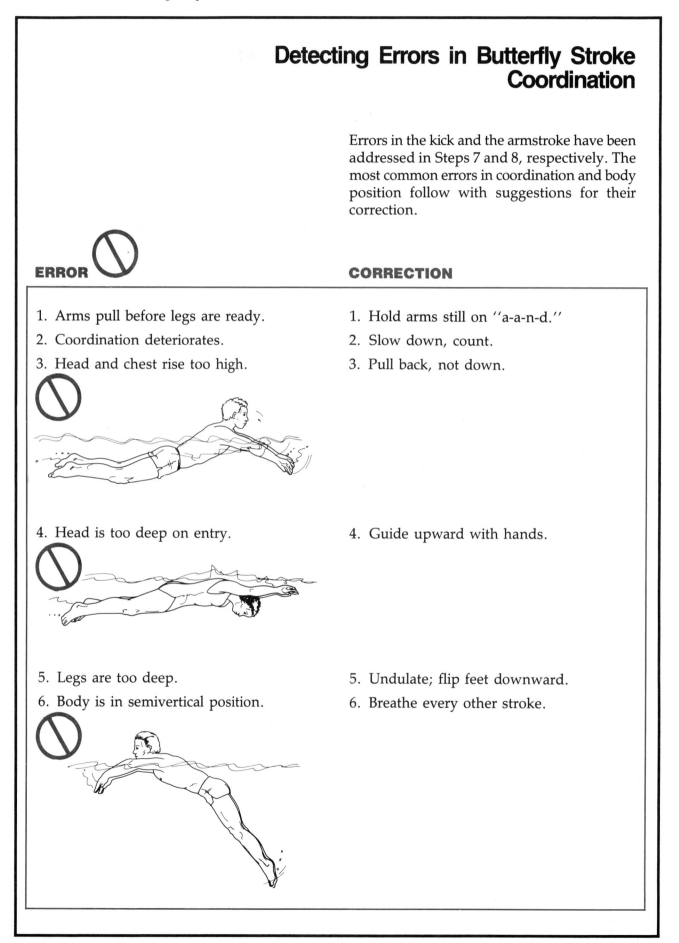

1. Arms pull before legs are ready.
2. Coordination deteriorates.
3. Head and chest rise too high.

1. Hold arms still on ''a-a-n-d.''
2. Slow down, count.
3. Pull back, not down.

4. Head is too deep on entry.

4. Guide upward with hands.

5. Legs are too deep.
6. Body is in semivertical position.

5. Undulate; flip feet downward.
6. Breathe every other stroke.

# Butterfly Stroke Coordination Drills

## 1. Paired Kick Drill With Fins

Goggles are optional, but don socks or boots and fins. Hold a kickboard in front of you with both hands. Begin kicking with the dolphin kick but stop after two downward kicks. Glide and slowly raise your feet and legs in preparation for the next pair of downward kicks. Continue to kick in pairs; kick downward rapidly twice and stop.

Begin to count downward kicks, saying ''one, and, two'' as your legs alternately kick downward, upward, and downward. Then, as you glide and your legs rise very slowly, say a long, drawn-out ''a-a-n-d.'' Thus, the count is ''1, and, 2, a-a-n-d.'' Take a breath during the long ''a-a-n-d'' count.

**Success Goal** = 50 yards or meters using paired dolphin kicks

**Your Score** = (#) _____ yards or meters using paired dolphin kicks

## 2. One-Armed Butterfly Stroke With Fins

Use fins; goggles are optional. Hold a kickboard at arm's length in front of you and keep your face in the water. Start kicking and counting in pairs as in Drill 1. During the glide at the end of the second pair of kicks, shift the kickboard to one hand and exhale. At the beginning of the third pair of kicks, pull with *one* arm, raise your head, and inhale. Start the pull slightly before you count ''one'' so the kick and inhalation come at midpull. Recover your arm over water on the count of ''and''; return it to the kickboard exactly on the count of 2. Leave both hands on the board during the long ''a-a-n-d'' count, and exhale.

Continue to stroke with one arm only, inhaling on the pull, for 50 yards or meters. Then change hands on the kickboard and pull 50 yards or meters with your other arm.

**Success Goal** =

50 yards or meters of one-armed butterfly stroke with each arm, with correct coordination

**Your Score =**

(#) _____ yards or meters of one-armed
butterfly stroke with each arm, with
correct coordination

## 3. *Butterfly Stroke With Fins, No Breathing*

Don fins and goggles. Do not use a kickboard. Start in a prone float position with arms extended overhead. Hold your breath and keep your face in the water while you raise your feet in preparation for a dolphin kick. Then pull with both arms on the first kick (Count 1). Recover your arms over the water as your legs rise again (Count ''and''). Make your arms enter the water overhead exactly on the second downward leg kick (Count 2). Glide. Hold your arms steady as your legs lift for the next stroke. Keep your face in the water and hold your breath as you swim two more strokes. Then stop, catch your breath, and begin again. Continue to swim three strokes at a time with your face in the water.

**Success Goal** = 5 sets of 3 non-breathing strokes with correct coordination

**Your Score** = (#) _____ sets of 3 strokes with correct coordination

## 4. *Butterfly Stroke With Fins, Alternate Breathing*

Wear goggles and swim fins. Start in prone float position with arms extended overhead. Raise your feet in preparation for a butterfly kick. Leave your face in the water and exhale as you kick twice and pull on the first stroke. On the second pull, tilt your head back, thrust your chin forward, open your mouth, and take a breath. Drop your face into the water and exhale during the third stroke; take a breath on the fourth.

Continue to swim butterfly stroke *slowly*, breathing on every second pull. Maintain your short arm glide (''a-a-n-d'') as your legs lift for the next stroke. Be very careful not to pull immediately as your hands enter the water.

**Success Goal** = 50 yards or meters of correctly coordinated butterfly stroke, breathing on alternate strokes

**Your Score** = (#) _____ yards or meters of correct butterfly stroke, breathing on alternate strokes

## 5. *Butterfly Stroke, Single Breathing*

Use swim fins and goggles. Swim butterfly stroke and take a breath at midpull on every stroke. Be careful not to lift your body and chest too high when you inhale. Stay as low as you can, pulling horizontally with a minimum of downward force. Tilt your head—don't lift it. Thrust your chin forward, not up, to get a breath. Remember to lift your legs during the long ''a-a-n-d'' count.

**Success Goal =** 50 yards or meters of correct butterfly stroke, breathing on every stroke

**Your Score =** (#) ____ yards or meters of correct butterfly stroke, breathing on every stroke

## 6. *Butterfly Stroke Without Fins*

Use goggles but no fins. Swim butterfly stroke. Swim slowly to get used to the loss of fins; it will seem strange, but persevere. Breathe on every stroke or every other stroke, as you wish. Avoid rising too high; try to keep your chin at water level. Be sure to maintain the glide of your arms as your feet rise for the next kick.

**Success Goal =** 50 yards or meters of correct butterfly stroke without fins

**Your Score =** (#) ____ yards or meters of correct butterfly without fins

## 7. *Refining the Rhythm of the Butterfly Stroke*

Swim butterfly stroke with goggles. Shorten the long ''a-a-n-d'' count to a simple ''and'' count, but be sure that your arms continue to stretch, not pull, during that count. Make the rhythm of the *kick* steady: 1, and, 2, and, 1, and, 2, and. Make the rhythm of the *armstroke* be this: 1, and, 2, reach, 1, and, 2, reach. Swim slowly, pulling all the way through.

**Success Goal =** 50 yards or meters of butterfly stroke with a steady, even rhythm

**Your Score =** (#) ____ yards or meters of butterfly stroke with a steady, even rhythm

# Butterfly Stroke Coordination Keys to Success Checklist

Steadiness of rhythm, fluidity of stroke patterns, and degree of rise and fall in the butterfly stroke cannot be assessed by counting the number of lengths you swim. An observer who knows what to look for must be the judge of such things. Ask a knowledgeable person to evaluate your butterfly stroke qualitatively according to the checklist within Figure 9.1.

## *Step 10*  **Butterfly Stroke Turn**

Because the butterfly stroke is used almost solely for competition, we will examine a butterfly stroke turn that is compatible with the competitive rules. The only rule governing the butterfly stroke turn states that both hands must touch the end wall simultaneously and that the shoulders must be on a level plane for the first armstroke after the turn. This turn is very efficient and will serve the noncompetitor, as well.

### WHY IS THE BUTTERFLY STROKE TURN IMPORTANT?

To a competitor all turns are very important. Many a race has been lost because of a poor turn. Because they incorporate a vigorous push from the wall, turns actually add to the speed with which a given distance may be covered. Turns are so important that competitors spend many practice sessions sharpening their turning technique. The noncompetitor benefits from competitive turns, as well, because they allow changing direction in a closed course with the greatest efficiency and the least disruption of the rhythm and fluidity of the stroke.

### HOW TO DO A BUTTERFLY STROKE TURN

Swim the butterfly stroke toward the end of the pool. Watch for the turn warning lines on the bottom of the pool and sight the end wall as you raise your head for a breath. Finish the stroke in progress as your head passes the turn line, bring your arms over the water on the recovery, and glide into the wall. *Use great caution to avoid hitting your head on the wall.*

Touch the wall with both hands simultaneously, tuck your knees tightly as you turn sideways to the wall, press with one hand on the wall to help bring your tucked legs under you as you raise your head, and pivot. Take your other hand from the wall and return it over the water to point toward the other end. As your feet move vertically under you toward the wall, bring your pressing hand over the water, begin to roll onto your stomach, take a breath, and put your face into the water.

As your feet touch the wall, push vigorously and extend your ankles to glide away in streamlined prone glide position under the water. Glide underwater until your speed decreases to top swimming speed, then begin kicking the dolphin kick to the surface. As your head is about to break the surface, resume the butterfly stroke, but do not breathe until the second stroke (see Figure 10.1).

## *Figure 10.1  Keys to Success: Butterfly Stroke Turn*

**Preparation Phase**

1. Judge distance from wall ____

2. Stretch arms forward after last pull ____

**Execution
Phase**

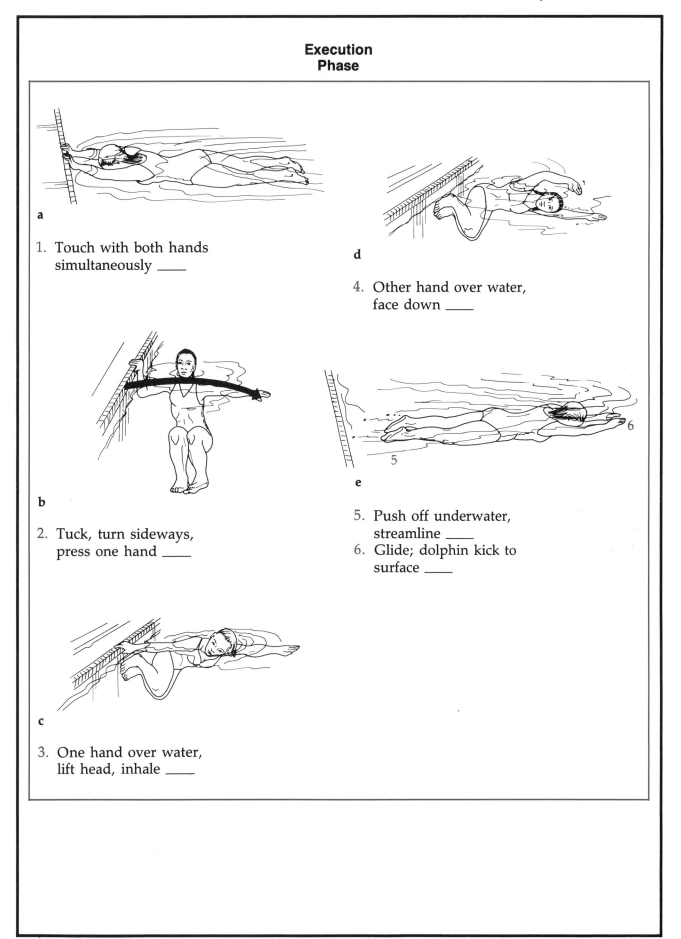

**a**

1. Touch with both hands
   simultaneously ____

**b**

2. Tuck, turn sideways,
   press one hand ____

**c**

3. One hand over water,
   lift head, inhale ____

**d**

4. Other hand over water,
   face down ____

**e**

5. Push off underwater,
   streamline ____
6. Glide; dolphin kick to
   surface ____

**Follow-Through Phase**

1. Resume stroke as head surfaces ____

2. Breathe on second stroke ____

## Detecting Errors in the Butterfly Stroke Turn

The butterfly stroke turn is quite simple, but mistakes do occur. Some of the common errors are listed here with suggestions on how to correct them.

**ERROR** ⊘

**CORRECTION**

| ERROR | CORRECTION |
| --- | --- |
| 1. You misjudge distance. | 1. Use short pull, or glide and kick in. |
| 2. You are too far from wall for push. | 2. Grasp edge, pull in. |
| 3. Push-off comes too early. | 3. Sink under first, then push. |
| 4. You stay on wall too long. | 4. Release wall before feet touch. |
| 5. Kick starts too early. | 5. Count to two while gliding. |
| 6. You lose momentum underwater. | 6. Start kicking after two counts. |
| 7. Breath is on first stroke. | 7. Keep face in water on first pull. |

## Butterfly Stroke Turn Drills

### 1. Judging Distance

This aspect of the turn is vital to your safety. Learn it well. As you approach the end of the pool, you must make a decision: take one more pull, or hold your glide and kick to the wall.

Wear goggles for this drill. Face the end of the pool, about 20 feet from the pool wall. Assume a prone glide position. Start the butterfly stroke. As your head passes over the turn target (the mark that is 5 feet or 2 meters from the end of the pool), complete the butterfly pull in progress and stretch your arms in front for a glide to the wall. If you find that you are still too far away from the wall to glide in without losing momentum, you may continue to kick until your hands touch the wall. If you think you have room for another armstroke before reaching the wall, try *cautiously* to take a small, quick, shortened stroke without pulling all the way through, then glide to the wall. Your glide should be about 2 feet. Practice judging your distance and your approach to the wall until you can approach at full speed with confidence and safety.

**Success Goal** = 10 consecutive full-speed approaches done safely and with confidence

**Your Score** = (#) _____ consecutive safe approaches with confidence

## 2. Choosing the Direction of Your Turn

Don your goggles and make a slow butterfly stroke approach to the end of the pool. As your hands reach the end of the pool, grasp the edge with both hands and pull in toward the wall as you tuck your legs and bring them in under you. Release the wall with your left hand and turn to your left, bringing your right side toward the wall. Throw your left arm back over the water to point to the other end of the pool. Push with your right hand to lift your head and start it going the other way. Grab a quick breath and release the wall as your tucked legs glide in under you to the wall. Bring your right arm over the water beside your left arm, and turn your face into the water as you turn onto your stomach and drop underwater.

As your feet touch the end wall with your legs tucked, push strongly and streamline for a glide underwater. Count to 2 while gliding, then start your dolphin kick to the surface. Resume stroking when you reach the surface. Do not breathe on the first arm pull.

Do this drill five times, then repeat it five times turning to the right, bringing the right hand away quickly and pushing with the left hand. Determine which direction you prefer.

**Success Goal** = determine preferred turn direction

**Your Score** = a preference for turning to the _____

## 3. Flat-Wall Turns

In the previous drill, you were instructed to grasp the edge of the pool and pull yourself into the wall. However, some pools have flat walls at the ends, with no edge to grasp. Practice making the turn with your palms touching flat against the end wall at water level.

Allow your elbows to bend as you glide in close to the wall. Then press sideways against the wall with your palms to initiate your turn. The rest of the turn is the same. Try the turn five times turning to the left and five times turning to the right.

**Success Goal** = 5 flat-wall turns in each direction

**Your Score** = (#) _____ turns in each direction

# Butterfly Stroke Turn
# Keys to Success Checklist

Even following a written description of a skill exactly does not guarantee that the skill will be done properly. Such things as relaxation, fluidity, and rhythm are not readily described.

Have a coach or a teacher use the checklist within Figure 10.1 to evaluate your skill in performing the butterfly stroke turn.

# Step 11 Improving the Breaststroke

The basic breaststroke is explained in *Swimming: Steps to Success*, Steps 17 and 18. Now the present, second-level text will review the kick and the armstroke and refine the coordination to bring it up to the competitive caliber.

## WHY IS THE BREASTSTROKE IMPORTANT?

Any stroke used in competition must be considered important in a second-level swimming text; the breaststroke is one of the four competitive swimming strokes. It is also thought to be one of the oldest strokes in the history of swimming. Its roots can be traced into biblical times and beyond. In his 1977 Ohio State doctoral dissertation titled *The History and Development of Men's Intercollegiate Swimming in the United States from 1897 to 1970*, D.F. Robertson stated ''that some form of breaststroke swimming was used by the Hebrews may be inferred from the following passage of Isaiah in the Bible: 'And he shall spread forth his hands in the midst of them as he that swimmeth spreadeth forth his hands to swim' '' (p. 12). It is thus the first in a series of strokes discussed in the next several steps of this text that will outline the evolution of swimming strokes.

## REVIEW OF THE BREASTSTROKE PULL AND KICK

This section reviews information from the basic-level text and gives an expanded explanation of the kick.

### Breaststroke Pull

Start from a prone float, arms extended. Flex your wrists, point your fingertips downward, and lift your elbows into the over-the-barrel position of the crawl stroke (see Figures 11.1a and b). Turn your hands to a slightly palms-out position. Lift your chin as you pull each arm sharply in a semicircular motion—out,

back, and in—with elbows bent 90 degrees and fingertips pointing directly downward (see Figure 11.1c). Breathe as you finish the pull with elbows out and palms up under your chin (see Figure 11.1d). To recover, drop your face back into the water, bring your elbows in to your sides, and turn your hands palm down and push them forward just under the water, fingertips leading, into full arm extension again (see Figures 11.1e and f).

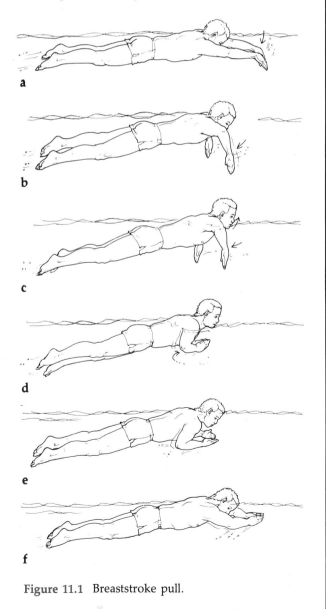

a

b

c

d

e

f

**Figure 11.1** Breaststroke pull.

The pull should feel as if you were fastening your fingertips into the water ahead and pulling your body through between them. Your elbows must remain as far forward as you can keep them until they are pulled to your sides. Propulsion should come from the palms of your hands pulling outward and back, and then inward and back to your chin. You complete the entire pull forward of your shoulders, and your hands should never pull past shoulder level. Each hand moves approximately in a small half circle from full extension to your chin.

### Breaststroke Kick

The breaststroke kick is nearly like the kick you use for the elementary backstroke, but it is inverted to prone position. Begin in prone glide position with legs straight and toes pointed. Allow your lower body to drop just low enough to keep your heels underwater as you bend your knees, hook your ankles, and lift your feet directly upward and forward as far as possible toward your buttocks. With both ankles hooked and your knees not spread more than shoulder width, turn your toes outward as far as possible (see Figure 11.2). From

Figure 11.2 Breaststroke kick.

this cocked position, move your feet outward to the sides and allow your knees to separate as you kick outward, around, back, and together again at full extension.

Try to feel the pressure of the water on the insides of your ankles at the start of the power phase. As your knees straighten, the pressure transfers to the bottoms of your feet, and you should extend your ankles to continue the pressure on the bottoms of your feet until they come together once again in full extension. Your heels should not break the surface, and your feet should move outward before your knees separate as you begin the kick. Avoid bringing your knees under you as you recover to the cocked position.

### BREASTSTROKE COORDINATION FOR COMPETITION

The coordination between the arm pull and the kick is slightly different for competition than it is for leisure swimming. The kick begins a little later in the stroke sequence, and the forward arm thrust begins earlier, resulting in a shorter glide.

From a prone float position, start the breaststroke arm pull and head lift. When the pull has been well started, bring both heels up behind you in the breaststroke kick recovery. Inhale quickly; as your hands rotate during the elbow squeeze, your feet should be rotating outward in preparation for the leg thrust. Drop your face down into the water and thrust your hands forward immediately, so they are nearly at full extension when the kick is at its most powerful. Streamline your body and prepare to begin the next pull with only a minimum stretch, which could hardly be called a glide. Exhale as you stretch forward with your arms (see Figure 11.3).

*Figure 11.3  Keys to Success:*
**Competitive**
**Breaststroke**

**Preparation
Phase**

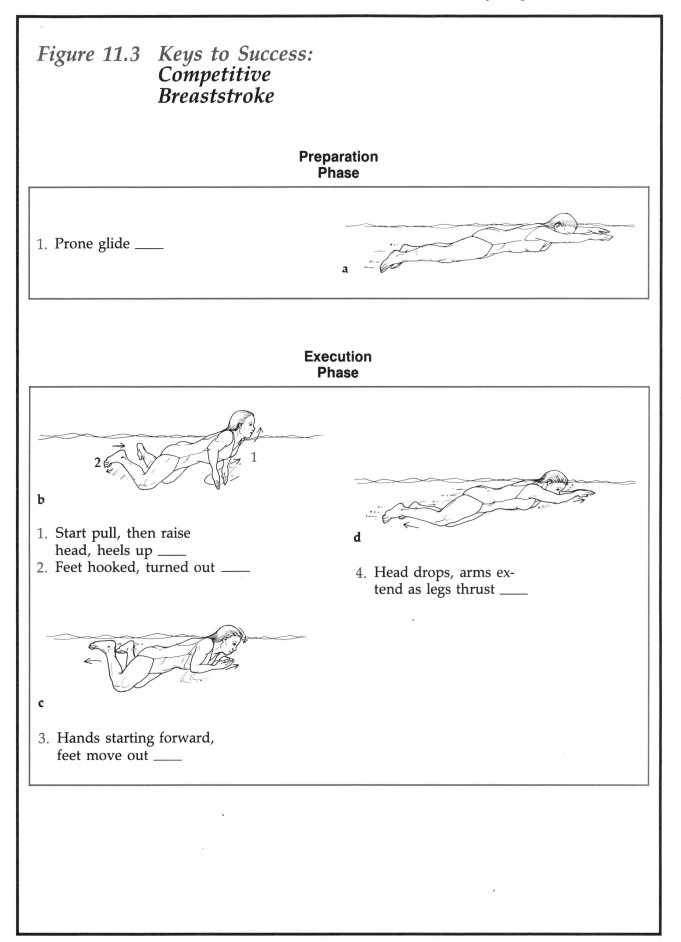

1. Prone glide ____

a

**Execution
Phase**

b

2   1

1. Start pull, then raise
   head, heels up ____
2. Feet hooked, turned out ____

d

4. Head drops, arms ex-
   tend as legs thrust ____

c

3. Hands starting forward,
   feet move out ____

**Follow-Through
Phase**

1. Head down, exhale,
   stretch for next stroke ____

# Detecting Errors in the Competitive Breaststroke

Learning to recognize a well-executed breast-stroke is easier if you can compare correct and incorrect technique. The most common breast-stroke errors follow, along with suggestions on how to correct them.

**ERROR**

**CORRECTION**

1. Coordination is lost.
2. Head and body rise too high.

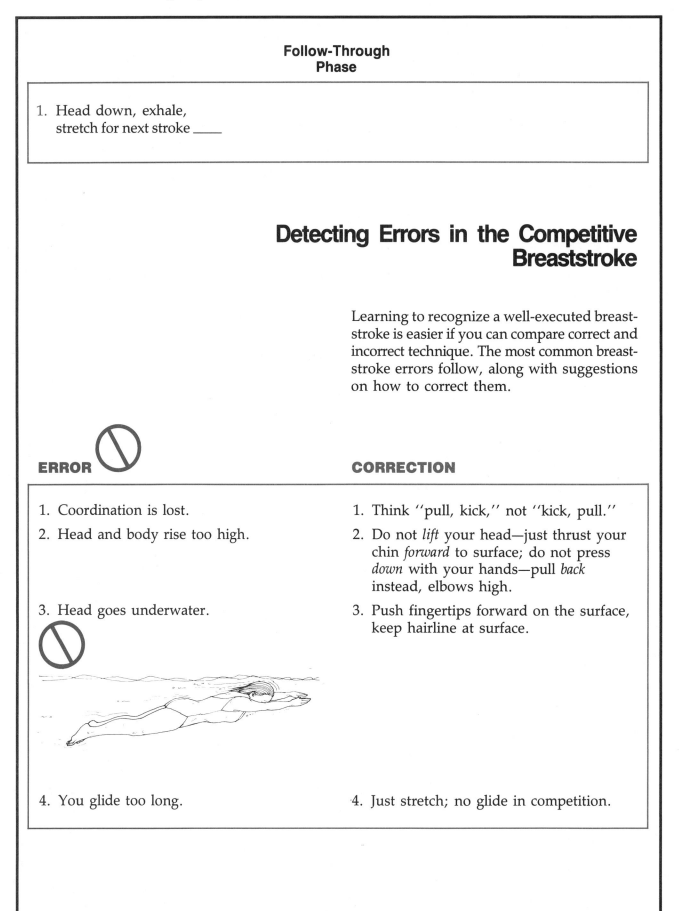

3. Head goes underwater.

4. You glide too long.

1. Think ''pull, kick,'' not ''kick, pull.''
2. Do not *lift* your head—just thrust your chin *forward* to surface; do not press *down* with your hands—pull *back* instead, elbows high.
3. Push fingertips forward on the surface, keep hairline at surface.

4. Just stretch; no glide in competition.

| ERROR | CORRECTION |
|---|---|
| 5. One foot turns in, engages water with top of foot.  | 5. Illegal kick—back to the drawing board! Drill, drill, drill on hooking the foot and turning toes outward on both feet. |

# Competitive Breaststroke Drills

## 1. Slow-Motion Breaststroke Pulls

In shallow water, hold a leg float between your knees. Put on your mask and your snorkel; this will allow you to concentrate more on the armstroke without worrying about breathing.

Practice stroking as described in the review section but without raising your head. Move your arms in very slow motion without thought of propulsion. Concentrate on correct arm and hand positions as you float.

**Success Goal =**

20 correctly executed slow-motion armstrokes while floating

**Your Score =**

(#) _____ correctly executed armstrokes

## 2. One-Arm Breaststroke Pulls

With a leg float between your knees, wear your mask and your snorkel. While holding a kickboard in one hand, float facedown; do not raise your head during this exercise. Move one arm through the breaststroke arm pull pattern in slow motion. Emphasize the high elbow position. Your forearm and hand should move in a semicircle, hanging down from a high, bent elbow. Keep your palm facing the direction of motion as it moves.

Shift the kickboard to your other hand to work with the opposite arm.

**Success Goal =**

30 practice pulls with each arm

**Your Score =**

(#) _____ practice pulls with each arm

## 3. Breaststroke Pulls for Propulsion

Use the leg-support float but neither mask nor snorkel. Emphasize gaining propulsion with these practice pulls. Dig in forcefully with your fingertips, then pull sharply and quickly with your forearms and hands to the position under your chin. Bring your elbows in; thrust your hands forward easily. Stop and glide. Take a breath, put your face down, and try again.

**Success Goal =** 40 quick, hard pulls with glide and breathing between

**Your Score =** (#) _____ quick, hard pulls with glide and breathing between

## 4. Coordinating Breaststroke Pulls With Breathing

Repeat Drill 3 but start by exhaling before the first pull. Then, using the pull of your hands to help, lift your chin forward until it is at water level. Open your mouth and inhale as your hands pull inward to your chin. At the end of the pull, while your elbows are squeezing inward, drop your face back into the water. Thrust your arms forward, then exhale on the glide. Be ready to lift your chin again on the next pull.

Be careful not to press down on the water more than is absolutely necessary to thrust your chin forward. Keeping your elbows high will help keep the pull in the right direction.

**Success Goal** = 25 yards or meters with successful breathing on every stroke

**Your Score** = (#) _____ yards or meters with successful breathing

## 5. Breaststroke Kick Bracket Drill

Grasp the top of the pool edge with one hand; position your other hand directly below, palm against the wall and fingers pointing to the bottom of the pool. By pulling on your top hand and pushing with your lower hand (gently), you can hold a position with your feet near the surface. If your body swings to one side, move your bottom hand slightly toward that side.

When comfortable in this bracket position, bring both heels up behind you in the breast-stroke kick recovery. Do not hold your feet so close to the surface that your heels come out of the water; allow your legs to sink far enough to keep your heels under. Practice the breaststroke kick in the bracket position, concentrating on the backward thrust with the insides of your ankles.

**Success Goal =**

feeling the thrust of your feet driving you against the wall

**Your Score =**

_____ thrust felt (yes or no?)

## 6. Breaststroke Kick Against Resistance

Repeat Drill 5 with someone standing behind you, placing his or her hands on the insides of your ankles, the fingers curling up over the soles of your feet. You kick against this resistance the hands provide. *CAUTION: Do not push very hard—these are weak muscles.*

**Success Goal =**

   feeling the pressure on the insides of
     your feet when you kick

**Your Score =**

   ____ pressure felt (yes or no?)

## 7. Breaststroke Kick With Kickboard

Holding a kickboard at arm's length with both hands, practice the breaststroke kick for propulsion. Keep your chin as low as possible to breathe. Do not bring your knees in under your body on the recovery; bring your heels up behind you. Your hips should not bend very much.

**Success Goal =** 25 yards or meters of breaststroke kick

**Your Score =** (#) ____ yards or meters of forward progress

## 8. Breaststroke Coordination With Mask, Snorkel

Float facedown on the surface with mask and snorkel. With absolutely no thought about propulsion, work on the coordination between arms and legs. Start lifting your heels before the pull begins. Hook your feet and point the toes out as the pull finishes. Your feet move outward while your elbows squeeze to your sides, and your arms are nearly fully extended, palm down, as the kick reaches full thrust. Do this drill in *very slow motion* while floating.

**Success Goal =** 40 slow-motion strokes

**Your Score =** (#) ____ slow-motion strokes

## 9. Breaststroke Coordination Without Mask, Snorkel

Repeat Drill 8 with neither the mask nor the snorkel. Hold your breath and keep your face down during the pull and kick. Exhale and take a new breath by raising your chin when your arms reach full extension, then keep your face in for the next stroke. Move *very* slowly. Do not try to move forward.

**Success Goal =** 40 slow-motion strokes

**Your Score =** (#) ____ slow-motion strokes

## 10. *Coordinating Breaststroke With Breathing*

Begin with a stretched prone float. Exhale, then begin to raise your head on the first stroke. Pull for propulsion, inhaling during the stroke. Drop your head back into the water as your hands come in under your chin. Exhale after the leg thrust as you stretch for the next stroke. Do one stroke at a time. Stretch while you concentrate on the beginning movements of the next stroke.

**Success Goal** = 20 strokes with easily coordinated breathing

**Your Score** = (#) _____ strokes

## 11. *Coordinated Breaststroke for Distance*

Start at one end of the pool. Swim breaststroke to the other end of the pool. Grasp the edge of the pool, tuck your legs, and pivot. Place your feet against the wall and push off. Hold your glide for 3 seconds before beginning the breaststroke again. Swim back to the starting end and repeat the wall turn. Continue swimming until you have swum 200 yards or meters.

**Success Goal** = 200 yards or meters of breaststroke

**Your Score** = (#) _____ yards or meters of breaststroke

## Competitive Breaststroke Keys to Success Checklist

It is important to swim for distance, but a qualitative judgment on how well you swim the stroke is also important. Someone who knows the stroke well should watch you swim and evaluate you according to the checklist within Figure 11.3.

# *Step 12*  **Breaststroke Turns**

The conventional breaststroke turn can be done two ways; competitive swimmers need to add an underwater stroke that recreational swimmers would find unnecessary and cumbersome. In either case, the turn is very similar to the butterfly stroke turn. You will learn both of these breaststroke turns and an alternative competitive breaststroke turn in this step.

## WHY ARE BREASTSTROKE TURNS IMPORTANT?

In a closed course it is sometimes a nuisance to have to break your stroke to turn at each end of the pool, but turning also increases your speed. It is important to turn smoothly with consistent, reliable efficiency and lack of stress. The breaststroke turns allow such ease.

## HOW TO DO CONVENTIONAL BREASTSTROKE TURNS

To turn easily when swimming for recreation, swim breaststroke toward the wall, gliding after each kick. When your head passes over the turn warning line or when it comes within 5 feet of the wall, complete the stroke then in progress with a kick and a glide. Streamline your body to glide with minimum loss of speed and touch the wall at water level with both hands simultaneously.

At the touch, allow your elbows to bend until your head is close to the wall. If the pool edge provides a handhold, grasp it and pull in quickly. Tuck your knees tightly and turn sideways to the wall, pulling one hand away and pressing with the other as your feet come in under you sideways toward the wall. Lift your head sideways, grab a breath, release the wall as or before your feet make contact, and place your face in the water facing the other direction. Put both hands under your chest, palms down and elbows in, and push off strongly, extending your arms to glide at or just under the surface. As your speed slows

to swimming speed, resume swimming the breaststroke.

For competition the turn is the same except for the addition of an underwater "pull-out" after pushing from the wall. Glide at a depth of about 2 feet. When your glide has slowed to swimming speed, pull strongly with both arms in a butterfly stroke all the way back until your thumbs rest against your thighs. Hold that arms-back streamlined position and glide again. As your speed once more slows to swimming speed, recover your legs for a breaststroke kick and recover your arms to a position under your chest. Kick vigorously, extending your arms forward to glide to the surface. As soon as your head breaks the surface, begin the breaststroke pull and resume stroking.

## HOW TO DO AN ALTERNATE BREASTSTROKE TURN FOR COMPETITION

Goggles are recommended. Start swimming breaststroke about 20 feet away from the end of the pool. Judge your approach to the end of the pool just as you did in the conventional turns. Glide with considerable momentum into the end wall, touching solidly with both hands simultaneously at water level.

At the touch, press strongly down and back with both arms as you tuck your legs tightly and bring both feet forward directly under you. Lay your head back on the water and inhale as your feet come through toward the wall. Pull your left hand to your chest with your elbow in tight. Meanwhile, turn your right hand palm up, hook your elbow, and lift up vigorously to roll to the right onto your stomach. Stay tucked and bring both hands to your chest with elbows in tight as you roll. As your feet contact the wall, push strongly with your legs, extend to glide position, and do the underwater stroke-and-kick "pull-out" for the competitive turn.

Of course, you may reverse the arm movements to roll to the left. Be careful not to hesitate after pressing with both arms and before lifting with one. The arm movement should be one continuous motion—down, turn, and lift—while the other arm presses down and is drawn immediately into the chest. Properly done, this turn is as fast as the conventional breaststroke turn and may be faster against a flat wall (see Figure 12.1).

## *Figure 12.1  Keys to Success: Breaststroke Turns*

**Preparation Phase**

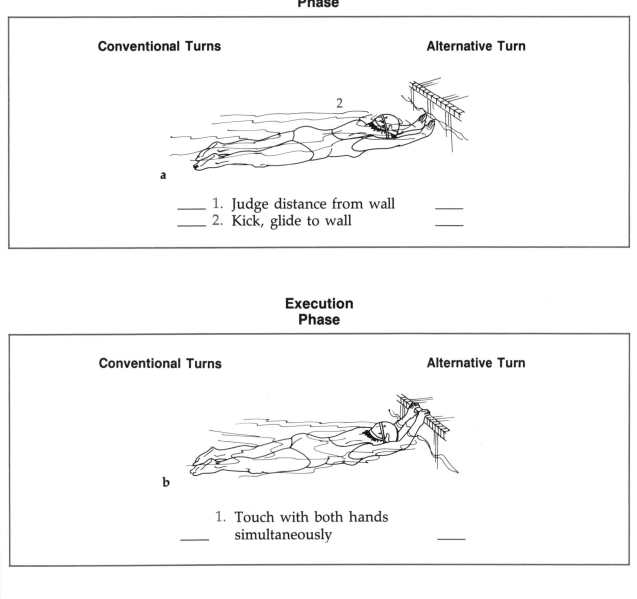

**Conventional Turns**                    **Alternative Turn**

a

_____ 1. Judge distance from wall        _____
_____ 2. Kick, glide to wall             _____

**Execution Phase**

**Conventional Turns**                    **Alternative Turn**

b

1. Touch with both hands
_____   simultaneously                    _____

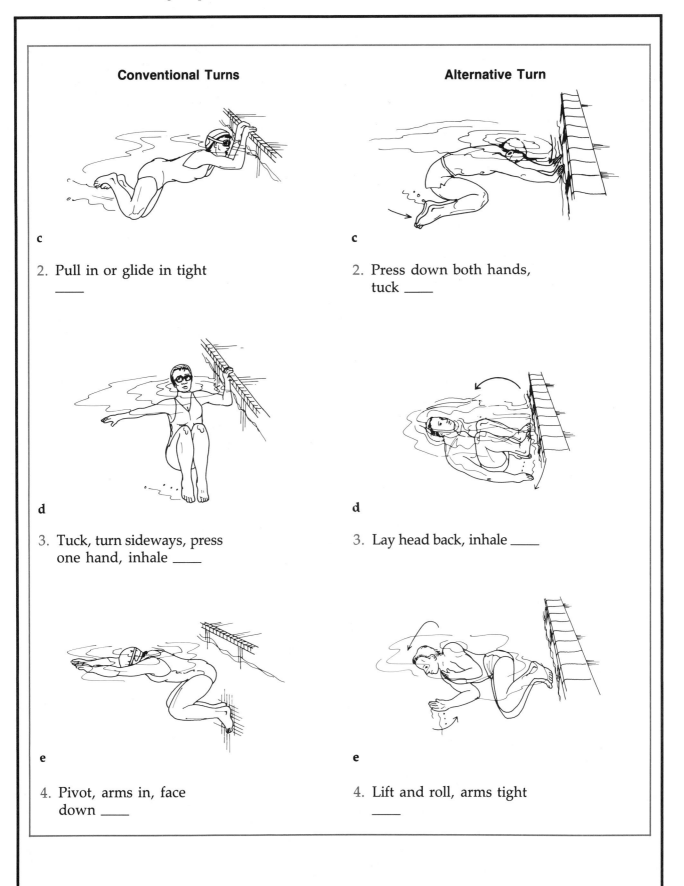

**Conventional Turns**

c

2. Pull in or glide in tight
____

d

3. Tuck, turn sideways, press
one hand, inhale ____

e

4. Pivot, arms in, face
down ____

**Alternative Turn**

c

2. Press down both hands,
tuck ____

d

3. Lay head back, inhale ____

e

4. Lift and roll, arms tight
____

**Conventional Turns**                    **Alternative Turn**

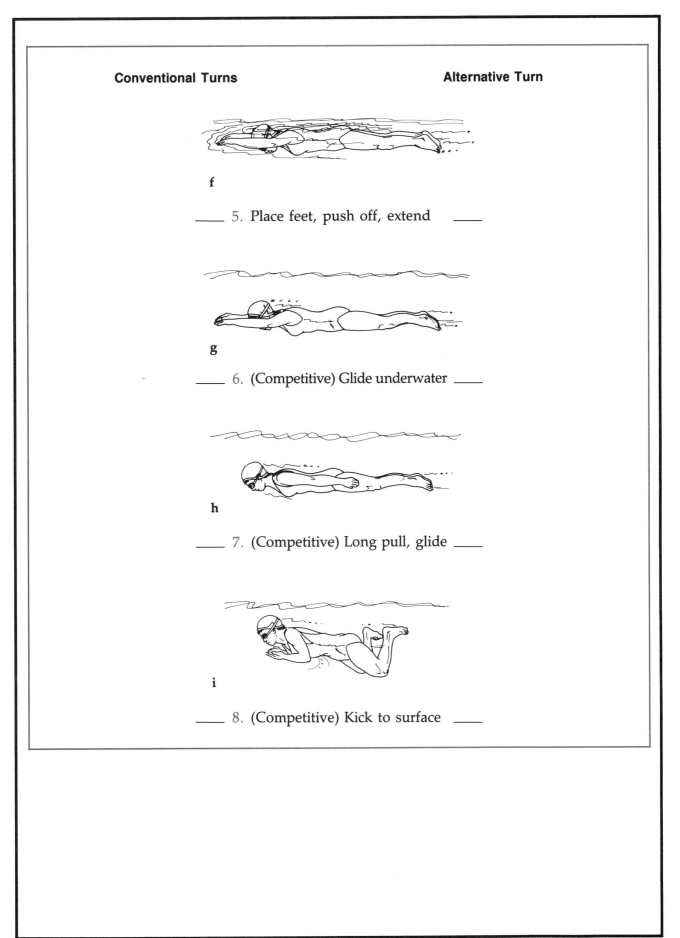

f

___ 5. Place feet, push off, extend  ___

g

___ 6. (Competitive) Glide underwater  ___

h

___ 7. (Competitive) Long pull, glide ___

i

___ 8. (Competitive) Kick to surface ___

**Follow-Through
Phase**

**Conventional Turns**                    **Alternative Turn**

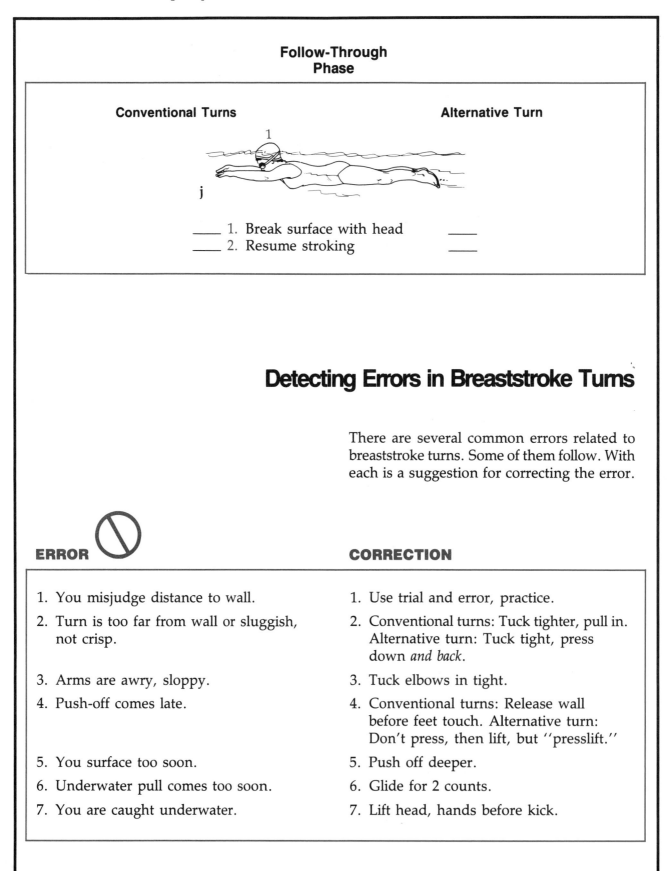

\_\_\_\_ 1. Break surface with head   \_\_\_\_
\_\_\_\_ 2. Resume stroking           \_\_\_\_

# Detecting Errors in Breaststroke Turns

There are several common errors related to breaststroke turns. Some of them follow. With each is a suggestion for correcting the error.

**ERROR**                                **CORRECTION**

1. You misjudge distance to wall.

2. Turn is too far from wall or sluggish, not crisp.

3. Arms are awry, sloppy.

4. Push-off comes late.

5. You surface too soon.

6. Underwater pull comes too soon.

7. You are caught underwater.

1. Use trial and error, practice.

2. Conventional turns: Tuck tighter, pull in. Alternative turn: Tuck tight, press down *and back*.

3. Tuck elbows in tight.

4. Conventional turns: Release wall before feet touch. Alternative turn: Don't press, then lift, but "presslift."

5. Push off deeper.

6. Glide for 2 counts.

7. Lift head, hands before kick.

# Breaststroke Turn Drills

## 1. Judging Distance for Conventional Breaststroke Turns

Wear goggles. Start swimming a moderate-speed breaststroke toward the end of the pool from about 20 feet. Watch for the turn line on the bottom of the pool or judge a distance of 5 feet from the wall. As your head passes the turn line or the spot you picked, finish the armstroke in progress, then kick exceptionally hard and streamline your body for a glide. Touch the wall with both hands simultaneously.

If you find that you slowed down perceptibly before touching, you must get a little closer for your last pull. Do that in one of two ways: Either glide a little longer on the next-to-last stroke or take an extra, very short armstroke after your head passes your mark. Practice the approaches until you can judge your position consistently to allow a final glide of 2 feet or less.

**Success Goal** = 5 consecutive approaches with a glide of 2 feet or less

**Your Score** = (#) _____ consecutive approaches with a glide of 2 feet or less

## 2. Conventional Recreational Breaststroke Turn

Wear goggles and start about 20 feet from the end wall. Make your approach as in Drill 1, but complete the turn as described in the how-to section, pushing off on or just under the surface and resuming your stroke after a short glide. Do not add the competitive underwater pull and kick described at the end of the how-to section. Do the turn in a slow, easy fashion without regard to speed.

**Success Goal** = 5 correct turns done smoothly and easily

**Your Score** = (#) _____ correct turns done slowly and easily

## 3. Conventional Competitive Breaststroke Turn

Wear goggles and use backstroke turn flags or a mark 15 feet from the end of the pool. Start swimming about 30 feet from the pool end wall. Do the turn as in Drill 2 but push off underwater and do the pull-out described for the competitive turns. Do the first five slowly, then add speed until you can turn in less than 9.0 seconds. Have someone time your turn from the second that your head passes the flags on the way in until your head passes the same point on your way out.

**Success Goal** = 5 turns done correctly, each in less than 9.0 seconds

**Your Score** = (#) _____ correct turns, each done in less than 9.0 seconds

# Alternate Breaststroke Turn Drills

## 1. Reversing in Midpool

Goggles are optional. You may wish to use a nose clip for the first few trials. Begin swimming breaststroke in midpool. As you glide in prone position, suddenly tuck your knees and press with both arms down and backward on the water, your legs shooting through under you and extending. You should end up on your back, headed in the opposite direction. Repeat the ''shoot-through'' several times, trying to make it crisp and sharp.

Then add this next movement: As you press down and back with your arms, pull one arm quickly in tight with your hand at your chest as you turn your other arm palm out, hook at the elbow, and lift, rolling yourself toward that arm and onto your stomach. Practice until the lifting arm moves in one continuous motion to press down and back, turn, and lift.

Try rolling in the other direction as well. Now as your feet shoot through, you should be rolling onto your stomach so you end up facing the opposite direction. Practice until you can reverse and roll crisply and sharply both to the left and to the right.

**Success Goal** = 5 consecutive crisp reverses to each side

**Your Score** = (#) _____ consecutive reverses to each side

## 2. Reversing at the Wall

Goggles are optional. You may wish to wear a nose clip until you learn to exhale a little through your nose as you roll. Start as for a midpool reverse (previous drill) but swim toward a pool wall. Glide to within a few inches of the wall and do a reverse and roll, but keep your legs tucked as you roll. When you are facedown, extend your legs carefully until your feet touch the wall, then push off with your toes.

If you find you are too far away to touch when you extend your feet, try to pull in toward the wall more as you press both arms down for the reverse. Practice until you can reach the wall with your feet consistently, rolling in each direction.

**Success Goal** = 5 consecutive reverses in each direction in which you reach the wall with your feet

**Your Score** = (#) _____ consecutive reverses in each direction

## 3. *Alternate Breaststroke Turn, Slow Motion*

Use a nose clip. Goggles are optional. Swim breaststroke very slowly toward a wall. Take a big breath and hold it as your hands glide to the wall. Touch the wall solidly with both hands simultaneously. Then initiate the alternate breaststroke turn *very slowly* as you float through a reverse and roll in *slow motion*. Hold your breath until you roll all the way onto your stomach. Think through each part of each motion until you feel you can do it at normal speed.

**Success Goal** = 10 slow-motion breaststroke turns

**Your Score** = (#) _____ slow-motion turns

## 4. *Alternate Breaststroke Turn for Speed*

Use goggles but no nose clip. Have a friend ready with a timer at the backstroke turn flags or another mark 15 feet from the end of the pool. Start swimming breaststroke about 30 feet from the end of the pool. Do the alternate breaststroke turn using the competitive underwater pull, the glide, the kick, the glide to the surface, and the resumption of swimming. Have your friend time you from the second that your head passes the turn flags on the way in until your head passes the same mark on the way out.

**Success Goal** = 5 time trials in which your time is under 9.0 seconds

**Your Score** = (#) _____ trials under 9.0 seconds

# Breaststroke Turns
# Keys to Success Checklist

Practice makes perfect only if you practice perfectly. Practicing the wrong way will not help—you already knew how to do it that way.

The checklist within Figure 12.1 will help your coach or teacher evaluate your turns for quality and legality.

# Step 13  Improving the Sidestroke

Ancient swimmers discovered that swimming the breaststroke with the head out of water was literally a pain in the neck. In an effort to ease the strain, they began to turn their heads to one side and put one ear on the water. Turning the head led to dropping one shoulder, and a new stroke gradually developed, using the same paired motions of arms and legs but rolling the body onto the side. The lateral motion of the legs, when turned onto the side, became the forward-back motion of the scissors kick. Thus was born the sidestroke, the second stroke in the evolution of swimming strokes. An alternative to the sidestroke, the overarm sidestroke, also evolved in the historical search for increased efficiency. Both of these strokes are presented in this step.

## WHY IS THE SIDESTROKE IMPORTANT?

The sidestroke was *the* competitive swimming stroke when it was proven to be faster than "belly swimming," as the breaststroke was once called. It, too, ultimately lost its place in competition, but it has never relinquished its reputation for being the workhorse of swimming strokes. It is important because it is the strongest stroke known for towing another swimmer for lifesaving purposes.

The sidestroke was introduced in the basic text, *Swimming: Steps to Success*, and is reviewed here because (a) it leads into the next evolutionary step in the history of swimming and (b) it belongs in a second-level text as the basis for lifeguard training.

## DEVELOPING STRENGTH IN THE SIDESTROKE

Improvement in the sidestroke depends upon attention to the details of the stroke, increasing the distance swum, and increasing the weight the stroke is called upon to support. We will briefly review the scissors kick, the sidestroke arm pull, and the sidestroke coordination.

### Review of the Scissors Kick

Hold a kickboard under one ear like a violin. Starting in a side glide position, bend at your knees and hips to bring both feet in a direct line toward your body (see Figure 13.1a). When your knees are fully bent (hips at 90 degrees), hook the top foot and step forward, as if to step onto a high step. At the same time, point the toes of your lower foot and step back as far as you can, as if to lay your toes on top of a large step behind you (see Figure 13.1b). Now step forward *and back* as far as you can as the legs thrust and squeeze, straightening to full extension (see Figure 13.1c). Point the toes of both feet during the thrust. Finish with feet together and streamlined. Turn the toes in slightly so they catch on each other at the finish. G-l-i-d-e.

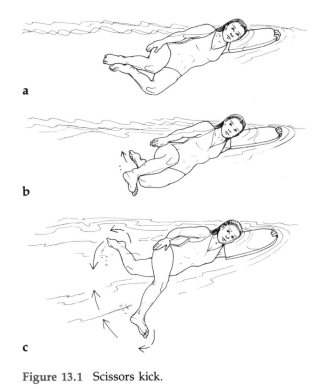

a

b

c

**Figure 13.1**  Scissors kick.

## Review of the Sidestroke Arm Pull

From a side glide position, lower arm extended forward under your head and upper arm along your side, flex your forward wrist to put the hand in position to pull back horizontally. Start the pull of the forward arm by bending your elbow and pulling back with your hand and forearm. Allow your hand and forearm to assume a horizontal position, your elbow bent 90 degrees, as you begin to pull from the shoulder. Pull as though you were gathering an armful of water and pulling it to your chest. When your forward elbow is pointing straight down, bring the hand up under your ear, turning it palm up. Squeeze your elbow to your side, point your fingertips forward, and fully extend your arm, palm up, just under the surface. Turn the palm down when your arm reaches full extension. Glide until ready for the next stroke.

Your upper, rearward arm moves in opposition to your forward arm. As the forward arm begins its pull, press the elbow of your other arm into your side; bend the elbow, bringing the top hand to your chin. Leave the palm down and keep the hand flat under the water as it moves. As your forward hand is turning palm up under your lower ear, bring your top arm forward to shoulder height and plunge your hand deep into the water in front of your face. Your top arm is now extended straight out from your shoulder; the elbow is bent 90 degrees, with the fingers pointing straight down at the bottom of the pool. As your forward arm extends to the starting position, your top arm pushes water, with the forearm and hand, directly backward toward your feet until it rests once again along your side. This returns your body to a streamlined position for the glide. Figures 13.2a to d show both the

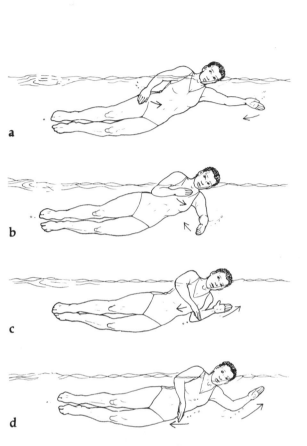

**Figure 13.2**  Sidestroke arm pull motions.

forward (lower) arm and rearward (upper) arm motions.

## Review of Sidestroke Coordination

From a side glide position, pull with your forward arm as your legs and your top arm recover. Thrust with the scissors kick and push with your top arm as your forward arm recovers. The kick coincides with the forward thrust of your forward arm, ending the stroke with power and in the streamlined position for a long glide. It should seem almost as though your top hand and your legs were tied together as they move in the same direction at the same time (see Figure 13.3).

*Figure 13.3  Keys to Success:*
*Sidestroke*
*Coordination*

**Preparation
Phase**

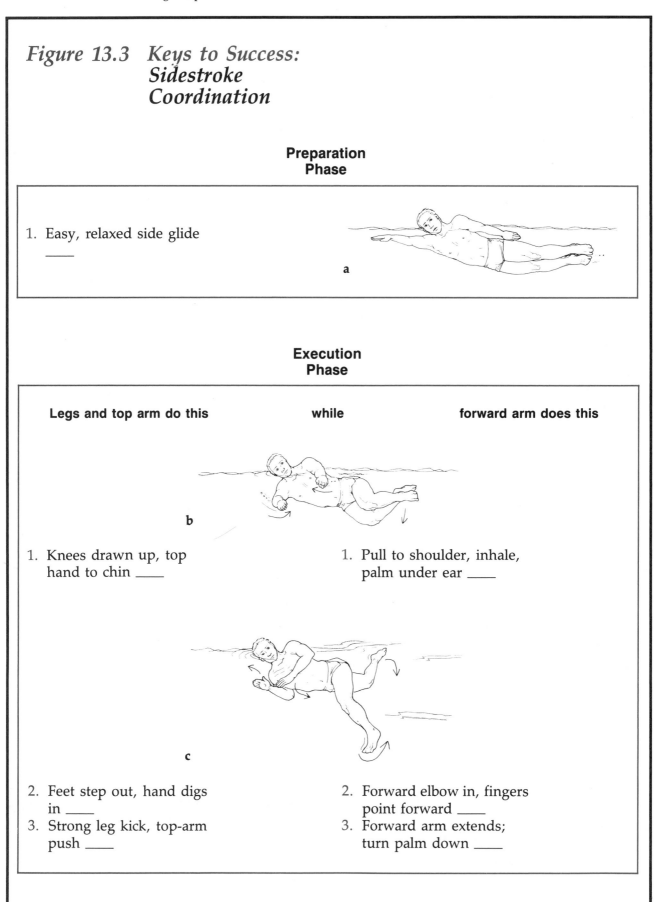

1. Easy, relaxed side glide
____

a

**Execution
Phase**

| **Legs and top arm do this** | **while** | **forward arm does this** |

b

1. Knees drawn up, top hand to chin ____

1. Pull to shoulder, inhale, palm under ear ____

c

2. Feet step out, hand digs in ____
3. Strong leg kick, top-arm push ____

2. Forward elbow in, fingers point forward ____
3. Forward arm extends; turn palm down ____

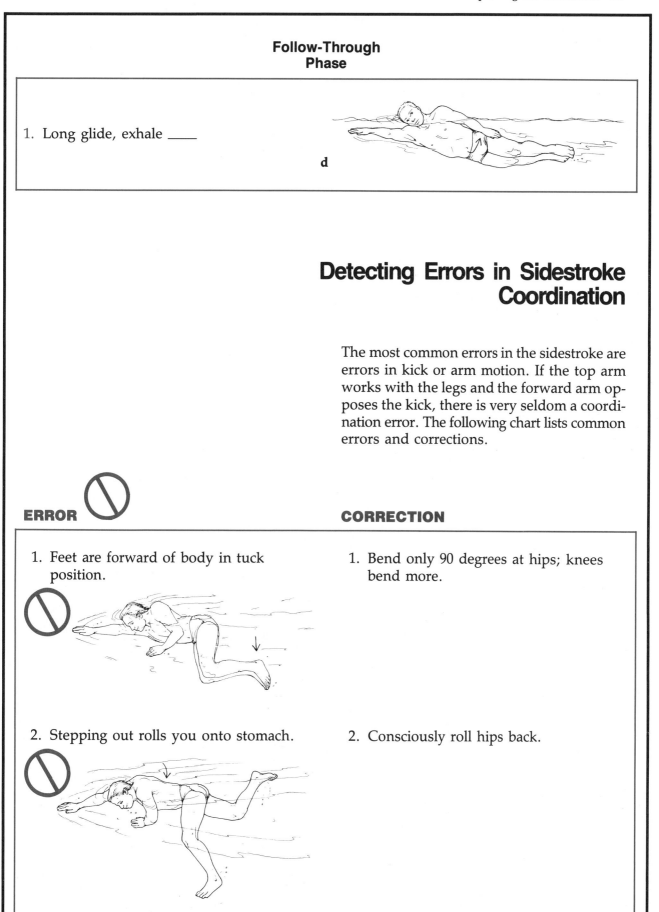

**Follow-Through
Phase**

1. Long glide, exhale ____

d

# Detecting Errors in Sidestroke Coordination

The most common errors in the sidestroke are errors in kick or arm motion. If the top arm works with the legs and the forward arm opposes the kick, there is very seldom a coordination error. The following chart lists common errors and corrections.

**ERROR**

**CORRECTION**

1. Feet are forward of body in tuck position.

1. Bend only 90 degrees at hips; knees bend more.

2. Stepping out rolls you onto stomach.

2. Consciously roll hips back.

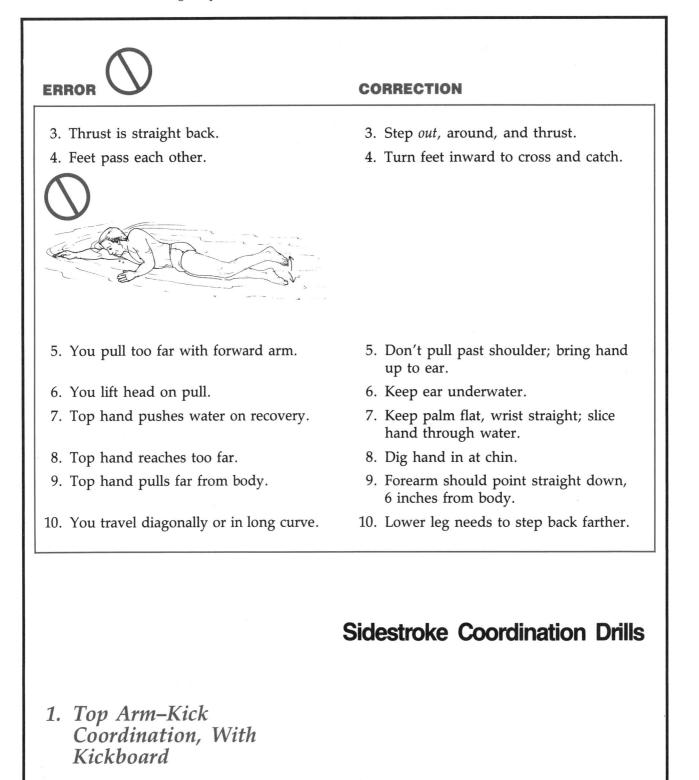

**ERROR**

**CORRECTION**

3. Thrust is straight back.

3. Step *out*, around, and thrust.

4. Feet pass each other.

4. Turn feet inward to cross and catch.

5. You pull too far with forward arm.

5. Don't pull past shoulder; bring hand up to ear.

6. You lift head on pull.

6. Keep ear underwater.

7. Top hand pushes water on recovery.

7. Keep palm flat, wrist straight; slice hand through water.

8. Top hand reaches too far.

8. Dig hand in at chin.

9. Top hand pulls far from body.

9. Forearm should point straight down, 6 inches from body.

10. You travel diagonally or in long curve.

10. Lower leg needs to step back farther.

# Sidestroke Coordination Drills

## 1. Top Arm–Kick Coordination, With Kickboard

Hold a kickboard at arm's length with your forward hand. Lay your top hand on the front of the thigh of your top leg. Do the scissors kick. Allow your elbow to bend as your legs recover, but keep your hand on your leg. During the thrust of the kick, press on your thigh with your hand as if to help it kick.

After the third or fourth kick, gradually remove your hand from your thigh; however, continue to make the same movement pattern with your hand 3 to 5 inches forward of your thigh. Keep the same coordination between hand and leg, but move your hand farther forward on each stroke until it is slicing to your chin and digging in to push on the water in correct sidestroke motion.

**Success Goal =**

    25 yards or meters, using scissors kick, top-arm push, and glide

**Your Score =**

    (#) _____ yards or meters

## 2. Forward Arm–Kick Coordination, With Kickboard

In sidestroke position, hold a kickboard under your top arm and near your top hip. From a glide position, pull with your forward arm and recover your legs for a scissors kick. Stop momentarily when your feet are ready to step out and your hand is under your ear. Check that everything is ready for a simultaneous leg thrust and arm extension to glide position. Then kick and reach into a long glide.

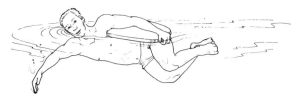

    Continue to hesitate at this coordination checkpoint for a few strokes. Then eliminate the hesitation and swim the stroke smoothly with a long glide.

**Success Goal =**

    40 forward-arm pulls and scissors kicks, smooth and coordinated

**Your Score =**

    (#) _____ coordinated pulls and kicks

## 3. Sidestroke Distance per Stroke

Push off the end wall and swim a fully coordinated sidestroke down the pool. Count your strokes. Try for an average of 6 feet or more per stroke.

**Success Goal** = 6 feet per stroke

**Your Score** = (#) _____ feet per stroke

## 4. 100-Yard Sidestroke

Swim a smooth, coordinated sidestroke, inhaling on the forward arm pull and exhaling on the glide.

**Success Goal** = 100 yards or meters of sidestroke, turning and pushing off at each end of the pool

**Your Score** = (#) _____ yards or meters

## 5. Lifesaving Sidestroke

Swim the sidestroke using only your legs and your forward arm. Use your top arm to hold a 10-pound diving brick or a similar-weight item on your top hip. Do not try to glide; alternate stroking and kicking continuously. Gradually increase the weight.

**Success Goal** =
    25 yards or meters carrying 10 to 15 pounds

**Your Score** =
    (#) _____ pounds carried for 25 yards or meters

## WHY IS THE OVERARM SIDESTROKE IMPORTANT?

The sidestroke was the fastest stroke known in the late 1800s; yet, competition sparked a search for still faster strokes with less negative motion. Recovering the top arm over the water reduced the negative motion of the sidestroke. In his book *How to Teach Swimming and Diving* (1934, p. 92), T.K. Cureton, Jr. quoted Archibald Sinclair as having said in *Swimming* (1909) that "the adoption by racing men of the style of progression known as the sidestroke ultimately led to the English side-overarm method of swimming." The overarm sidestroke is presented here as the third in the evolutionary series leading to the present-day crawl stroke.

## HOW TO SWIM THE OVERARM SIDESTROKE

Begin by swimming an easy, relaxed sidestroke. Notice that your upper arm pushes forward underwater on the recovery, resisting your body's forward movement. Pull through a stroke and glide.

Now lift your upper arm just above the water, keeping your elbow close to your side. Bend the elbow and slice your hand over the water, palm down, toward your face. As your hand reaches shoulder level, lift your elbow and bring the forearm in front of your face with your elbow bent at a right angle. As your hand reaches the level of your eyebrows, let your upper arm continue to come forward but drop your forearm and hand to point vertically downward in front of your forehead. Your forearm, straight wrist, and hand should enter the water vertically and begin to push backward toward your feet.

Push with the kick exactly as you would for a conventional sidestroke. The timing and the coordination also remain the same. The only change from the conventional sidestroke is that one arm recovers over the water. Continue the overarm sidestroke with your upper arm entering the water at eyebrow level (see Figure 13.4).

## Figure 13.4   Keys to Success: Overarm Sidestroke

**Preparation Phase**

1. Swim sidestroke, glide
——

a

## Execution Phase

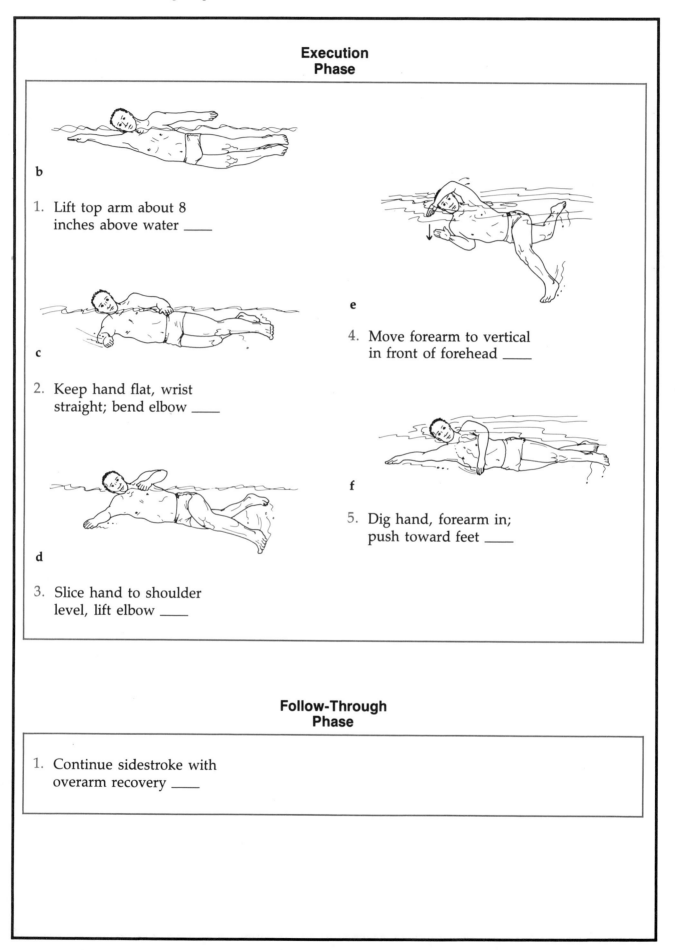

b

1. Lift top arm about 8 inches above water ____

c

2. Keep hand flat, wrist straight; bend elbow ____

d

3. Slice hand to shoulder level, lift elbow ____

e

4. Move forearm to vertical in front of forehead ____

f

5. Dig hand, forearm in; push toward feet ____

## Follow-Through Phase

1. Continue sidestroke with overarm recovery ____

# Detecting Errors in the Overarm Sidestroke

The following errors relate only to the overarm recovery. Other sidestroke errors can be found earlier in this step.

**ERROR**                                    **CORRECTION**

1. Recovery is too high.                     1. Keep hand 6-8 inches over water.

2. Hand is too far from body.                2. Keep elbow in tight until hand reaches shoulder level.

3. You overreach.                            3. Brush forehead with thumb.

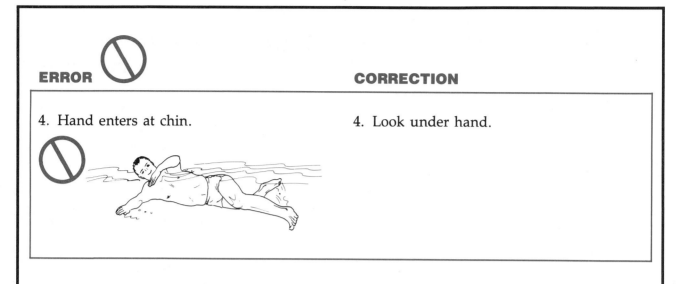

ERROR 🚫                                          CORRECTION

4. Hand enters at chin.                           4. Look under hand.

# Overarm Sidestroke Drills

## 1. Top Arm and Kick, With Kickboard

Goggles are optional. Assume a sidestroke glide position while holding a kickboard under your ear (like a violin) with your lower (forward) arm; your top (rearward) arm lies along your side. Begin doing the scissors kick, gliding after each kick.

   After the third or fourth kick, add the sidestroke upper-arm pull in coordination with the kick, but recover it *over* the water as described in the how-to section. Be sure to carry your arm to your forehead before the forearm enters vertically for the backward thrust. The recovery and thrust should coincide with the recovery and thrust of the top leg. Take a long glide after each stroke.

**Success Goal** = 100 yards or meters using correct overarm recovery and coordination

**Your Score** = (#) _____ yards or meters

## 2. Overarm Sidestroke

Swim a normal sidestroke. Pay particular attention to coordination and glide. Note that your upper arm causes considerable resistance on the recovery even though the hand slices sideways.

   From a standpoint of efficiency (competitive swimmers, read "speed"), a longer stroke and less resistance is desirable. Now lift your upper arm over the water and reach forward to your forehead before placing your hand in the water for a push. Swim the overarm sidestroke but don't change the coordination. Note the increase in efficiency (and speed, if you care to time it).

**Success Goal =** recognize the increased efficiency during 100 yards or meters of over-arm sidestroke

**Your Score = _____** the extent to which you realize this increased efficiency

# Improving the Sidestroke Keys to Success Checklists

The sidestroke lends itself to the quantitative assessment of power through measurements of weight and distance. That still doesn't measure confidence, relaxation, and fluid dynamics, which can be measured only qualitatively. If you do not recognize an increase in effi-ciency when using the overarm sidestroke, perhaps your technique is faulty. Ask someone knowledgeable to evaluate your side-stroke and your overarm sidestroke according to the checklists within Figures 13.3 and 13.4, respectively.

# *Step 14* **Trudgen Strokes**

The search for increased efficiency and speed that led to the overarm sidestroke led to the next three strokes in the evolutionary process, variations of efforts to eliminate water resistance by recovering both arms over the water. In his 1934 book, *How to Teach Swimming and Diving*, T.K. Cureton, Jr. writes that ''[John] Trudgen demonstrated the important principle of recovering both arms free of the water, and greatly increased the interest in competitive swimming'' (p. 94). The three strokes that bear his name are the trudgen stroke, the double trudgen, and the trudgen crawl. You will learn all three in this step.

## WHY IS THE TRUDGEN STROKE IMPORTANT?

The trudgen stroke is a key link in the evolution of strokes from the breaststroke to the crawl, and it is swum by many swimmers today who think they are doing the crawl. It is an easy, restful version of the overhand stroke. As such, it has importance in its own right, but it is still three evolutionary steps from the crawl.

## HOW TO SWIM THE TRUDGEN STROKE

Start in a prone float position with both arms stretched overhead. Begin a normal crawl pull with your breathing-side arm and roll your head to take a breath. As your arm begins to pull, roll your hips to face toward the pulling arm and recover your legs for a standard scissors kick (top leg forward). As your hand reaches waist level, begin the power phase of the kick and inhale. Make your armstroke and scissors kick finish together. Allow your legs to relax, but keep your feet together, as you turn your face into the water and recover your breathing-side arm. Then exhale during a complete crawl armstroke with the opposite arm, legs resting.

Thus, you recover your legs and deliver a scissors kick while pulling with one arm, then allow your legs to relax and rest during the other arm pull. Use normal crawl stroke coordination for the arms: One arm starts when the other is about to enter the water. The delivery of power is uneven, and the stroke will appear to be somewhat jerky: You surge ahead while breathing and kicking (see Figure 14.1).

*Figure 14.1 Keys to Success:*
*Trudgen Stroke*

**Preparation**
**Phase**

1. Prone float, arms overhead ____

**Execution
Phase**

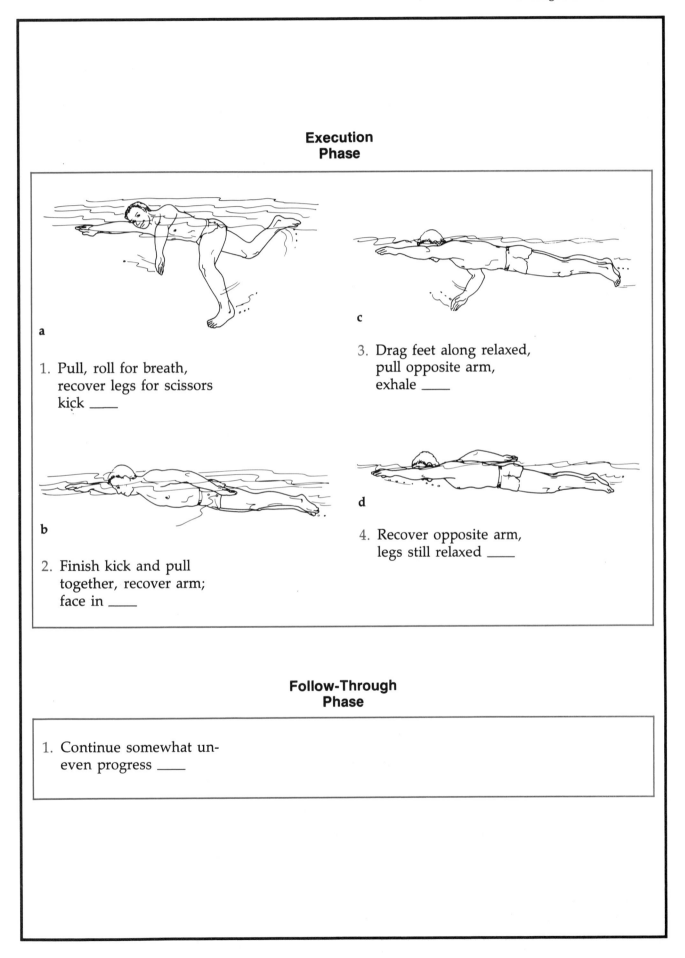

a

1. Pull, roll for breath,
   recover legs for scissors
   kick ____

b

2. Finish kick and pull
   together, recover arm;
   face in ____

c

3. Drag feet along relaxed,
   pull opposite arm,
   exhale ____

d

4. Recover opposite arm,
   legs still relaxed ____

**Follow-Through
Phase**

1. Continue somewhat un-
   even progress ____

# Detecting Errors in the Trudgen Stroke

Some common errors encountered in the trudgen stroke are detailed here. Use the accompanying suggestions for corrections.

**ERROR** 🚫

**CORRECTION**

| ERROR | CORRECTION |
|---|---|
| 1. You breathe on wrong side. | 1. Always breathe on the kick. |
| 2. Feet cause resistance. | 2. Keep feet together, relaxed. |
| 3. You have coordination problems. | 3. Do one sidestroke, one crawl. |
| 4. Scissors kick is inverted. | 4. Always move top leg forward. |

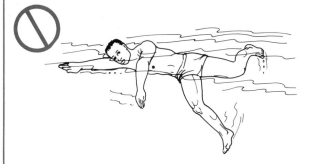

| ERROR | CORRECTION |
|---|---|
| 5. Kick takes too long. | 5. Use narrower kick. |

# Trudgen Stroke Drills

## 1. Overarm Sidestroke, Overreaching

If a longer pull with the upper arm in the overarm sidestroke contributed to greater efficiency, then an even longer stroke might make it even more efficient. Swim an overarm sidestroke. Maintain the same coordination and glide after each stroke. However, begin slowly, bit by bit, to reach farther forward with your upper arm; place your upper hand in the water near the top of your head, then reach a little farther on the next stroke. Continue until you are reaching just as far for the entry as you do on a crawl stroke entry. As you reach and pull longer, you will find that you must roll farther onto your stomach for the entry.

As you reach farther forward, the pull will take longer, and your kick will not fit the coordination pattern as well. Delay the recovery of your legs until your upper arm begins to pull. Thus, you will not bring your legs up until the end of your lower-arm pull and the beginning of the upper-arm pull. Because your legs must now both recover and kick on one armstroke, you have to narrow the kick somewhat to speed it up. Recover your legs and kick on the upper-arm pull, as your lower arm moves forward for the glide.

**Success Goal** = 25 yards or meters of overarm sidestroke with the upper hand reaching as far forward as a crawl stroke entry

**Your Score** = (#) _____ yards or meters of overarm sidestroke

## 2. *Overarm Sidestroke, Extended Lower-Arm Pull*

Swim overarm sidestroke, overreaching to full extent with your upper arm and both recovering and kicking your legs on the pull of your breathing-side arm. As you swim, begin also pulling farther with your lower arm on each stroke. Continue to recover and kick your legs while your breathing-side arm pulls and the lower arm shoots forward for the glide. Because you have delayed the leg recovery, your legs do absolutely nothing during the lower-arm pull but rest and drift.

When you reach the stage where your lower arm is pulling all the way to your thigh, you will find that you must roll completely onto your stomach during the pull of your lower arm while your breathing-side arm is recovering. Because you are already on your stomach when your lower arm finishes, it would be easy to lift your lower arm over the water as in a crawl stroke recovery. Do it. Delay the pull of your breathing-side arm until your lower arm has nearly finished its recovery. Your legs will just continue to drag because they do not start to recover until your breathing-side arm starts to pull.

Now the stroke should begin to look like a crawl stroke, but everything happens on one side. While your breathing-side arm pulls, breathe, recover, and kick your legs. As your other arm pulls and recovers, your legs remain still and rest. So, do a sidestroke on one side and a crawl stroke with the other arm.

**Success Goal** = maintain correct coordination through 25 yards or meters

**Your Score** = (#) _____ yards or meters

## 3. *Trudgen Stroke Drill*

Swim crawl stroke without kicking your feet; let your legs relax and drag. Do two strokes with each arm. Then, as you begin to pull with your breathing-side arm, turn your hips slightly to face that side. During the first half of the arm pull, recover your legs in preparation for a narrow, standard scissors kick (top leg forward). During the second half of the pull, deliver the narrow scissors kick. Allow your legs to drag as you recover that arm; pull and recover the other arm. Swim a crawl stroke with a scissors kick on the breathing side. This is the trudgen stroke, refined from the stroke introduced in England by John Trudgen in the early 1900s.

**Success Goal** = 100 yards or meters of correct trudgen stroke

**Your Score** = (#) ____ yards or meters trudgen stroke

## WHY IS THE DOUBLE TRUDGEN STROKE IMPORTANT?

At one point in the trudgen stroke, your legs are dragging while one arm pulls. If you add a second scissors kick to the coordination of the stroke, you will be doing the double trudgen stroke. It is the most powerful of the overhand strokes, though not the fastest. It has important uses in lifesaving and in surf swimming, where it may be important to keep your head high to see.

## HOW TO SWIM THE DOUBLE TRUDGEN STROKE

Begin swimming the trudgen stroke. Notice the ''dead space'' in the leg kick during the pull of your non-breathing-side arm. After delivering a kick and a stroke on your breath-ing side, immediately rotate your hips and recover your legs on the opposite side for a scissors kick with your other armstroke. The kick must also be a standard kick (top leg forward), so your opposite leg must step forward. Deliver the kick during the last half of that arm pull.

In sum, pull with your left arm as you deliver a scissors kick facing to the left with your left leg forward. Next pull with your right arm as you deliver a scissors kick facing to the right with your right leg forward. In effect, you are doing a sidestroke, rolling and alternating sides for each stroke. Breathe only on one side, exhale on the other. Each kick is powerful, and you will surge through the water with each stroke. You will find that you can carry your head out of water better with this stroke than any other (see Figure 14.2).

*Figure 14.2  Keys to Success:*
***Double Trudgen Stroke***

**Preparation
Phase**

1. Swim trudgen stroke ____

## Execution
## Phase

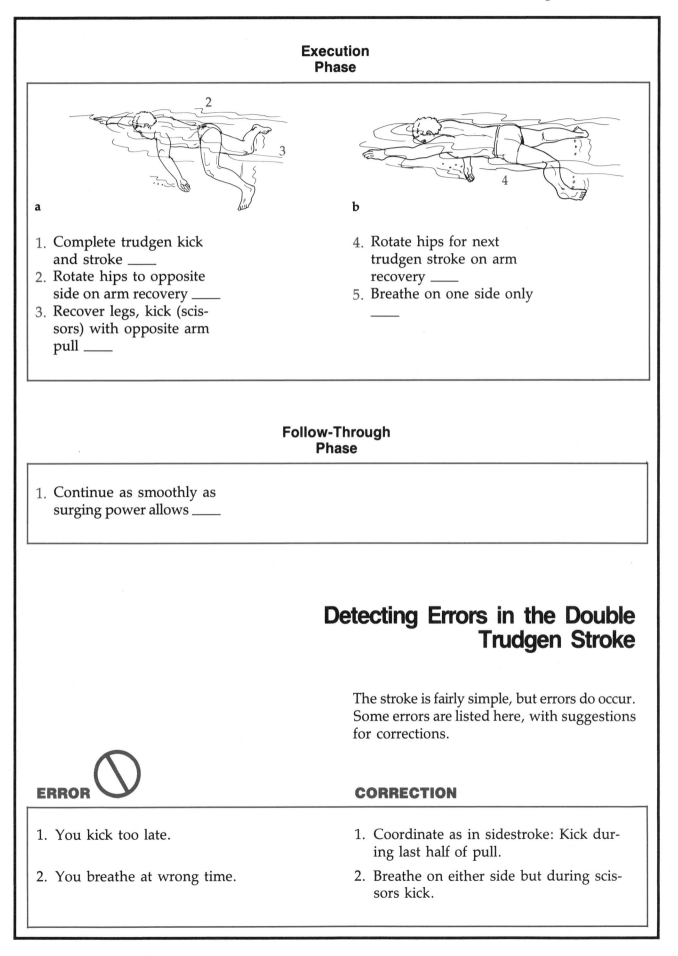

**a**

1. Complete trudgen kick and stroke ____
2. Rotate hips to opposite side on arm recovery ____
3. Recover legs, kick (scissors) with opposite arm pull ____

**b**

4. Rotate hips for next trudgen stroke on arm recovery ____
5. Breathe on one side only ____

## Follow-Through
## Phase

1. Continue as smoothly as surging power allows ____

# Detecting Errors in the Double Trudgen Stroke

The stroke is fairly simple, but errors do occur. Some errors are listed here, with suggestions for corrections.

**ERROR** 🚫

**CORRECTION**

1. You kick too late.

1. Coordinate as in sidestroke: Kick during last half of pull.

2. You breathe at wrong time.

2. Breathe on either side but during scissors kick.

| ERROR 🚫 | CORRECTION |
|---|---|
| 3. There is great resistance on kick. | 3. Make kick smaller, narrower. |
| 4. You have excessive jerkiness. | 4. Soften kick. |
| 5. You get fatigued. | 5. Glide after each stroke. |

# Double Trudgen Stroke Drills

## 1. Double Trudgen Kick Drill

Start in a prone float position with a kickboard in both hands at arm's length. Do scissors kicks, alternating sides. Be sure that your top leg moves forward on each side. This requires that your right leg leads when you are facing right (a), and your left leg leads when you face left (b). Inhale on one kick; leave your face in the water and exhale on the other kick.

a

**Success Goal =**

   50 yards or meters with smooth
     transition from one side to the other

b

**Your Score =**

   (#) ____ yards or meters with smooth
     transitions from one side to the other

## 2. One-Arm Stroke, Double Trudgen, With Kickboard

Start double trudgen scissors kicks while holding a kickboard with both hands. After two sets of kicks, start pulling with one arm while your legs recover for a kick. Deliver the kick during the last half of the arm pull, then return

that hand to the board. Leave both hands on the kickboard while you kick on the other side. Then pull again with the same arm on the next kick.

Continue pulling with only one arm for 25 yards or meters, then shift to pull with the other arm on the other side with the other kick. Slow down enough that you can be sure the kick comes during the last half of the arm pull.

**Success Goal =**

25 yards or meters with each arm
   properly coordinated

**Your Score =**

(#) ____ yards or meters with each arm
   properly coordinated

## 3. Double Trudgen Stroke, Both Arms, With Kickboard

Hold a kickboard in both hands at arm's length. Begin alternate-side scissors kicks. Pull with your left arm during a left-side kick, then return your hand to the kickboard and glide. Next pull with your right arm during a right-side kick, then return that hand to the board and glide. Continue pulling and kicking alternately on the left and right sides, with a glide following each stroke.

**Success Goal =** 50 yards or meters of alternate stroking with glides

**Your Score =** (#) ____ yards or meters of alternate stroking with glides

## 4. Double Trudgen Stroke

Begin with a prone glide. Begin a crawl stroke pull and a scissors kick on each side, alternating sides continuously. Take a short glide after each stroke. Inhale during one stroke, exhale during the other. You may carry your head up all the time or drop your face into the water during one arm pull.

**Success Goal =** 100 yards or meters of well-coordinated double trudgen stroke

**Your Score =** (#) ____ yards or meters of well-coordinated double trudgen stroke

## WHY IS THE TRUDGEN CRAWL STROKE IMPORTANT?

The trudgen crawl stroke is similar to the double trudgen stroke, except that the kick is different. Instead of two scissors kicks, the trudgen crawl stroke employs one scissors kick and three flutter (crawl) kicks.

T.K. Cureton, Jr. again provides us with historical background. In his 1934 book, *How to Teach Swimming and Diving*, he wrote that "some of the American coaches were reluctant to give up the wide 'scissors' kick of the trudgen stroke. [Frank] Sullivan experimented with a stroke which combined the features of the trudgen and the crawl. The stroke became known as the trudgen-crawl and was characterized by a series of flutter kicks added to the wide major kick of the trudgen" (p. 97).

## HOW TO SWIM THE TRUDGEN CRAWL STROKE

The trudgen crawl inserts three smaller crawl kicks in place of the second scissors kick of the double trudgen. Thus, your leg rhythm is slash, beat, beat, b-e-a-t, slash, beat, beat, b-e-a-t—where "slash" is a scissors kick and the long "b-e-a-t" is the recovery for the next scissors. The slash comes at the end of one arm pull, and the other arm pulls during the three flutter kicks.

Breathe on the scissors kick, as with the trudgen stroke. Keep your face in the water and exhale during the pull and flutter kicks. Keep the scissors kick small, not much more than a large flutter kick. In fact, if you narrow the scissors kick to the same size as a flutter kick, it *becomes* a flutter kick and you would be swimming the 4-beat Australian crawl. The sidestroke would then have evolved into a crawl stroke. Adding two more leg kicks in the coordination pattern would make it the standard American crawl.

# Detecting Errors in the Trudgen Crawl Stroke

Errors in the stroke usually occur at the same points as in the double trudgen. Some errors are listed here, with suggestions for corrections.

**ERROR**

**CORRECTION**

1. You do scissors kick on arm recovery.

1. Keep sidestroke coordination: Kick during last half of pull.

| ERROR ⊘ | CORRECTION |
|---|---|
| 2. You breathe on wrong side. | 2. As in sidestroke, inhale on scissors kick. |
| 3. Leg recovery takes too long. | 3. Make kick narrower. |
| 4. You have excessive jerkiness. | 4. Slow down, pull through. |

# Trudgen Crawl Stroke Drills

## 1. Trudgen Crawl Kick, With Kickboard

Start in a prone float position, holding a kickboard in both hands at arm's length. Rotate your hips to face the left side. Recover your legs; step forward with your left leg, back with your right leg. Then do a scissors kick but allow your feet to pass each other at the end of the kick (count "slash" as you kick). As you deliver the kick, roll back to a prone position. Do three crawl stroke (flutter) kicks, counting "beat, beat, beat" as they kick (left foot kicking downward on the first, right foot kicking down on the second, and left foot kicking down again on the third).

As you begin the third crawl kick, roll again facing left and extend the third beat into a recovery for another scissors kick. If you counted properly, the left foot will be moving forward on the third beat, so the recovery for a scissors kick will be with your left foot leading as in the first scissors kick. Extending the third beat into a scissors kick recovery will slow the third beat, so the rhythm now becomes slash, beat, beat, b-e-a-t, slash, beat, beat, b-e-a-t. Keep this kicking rhythm for 25 yards or meters, inhaling on the scissors kick and exhaling with your face in the water on the three flutter kicks.

Change to do the scissors kick facing right instead of left. The right leg now moves forward on the recovery for the scissors kick. Also, you now inhale on the right side during the scissors kick and exhale with your face down on the three flutter kicks. Continue kicking facing to the right for 25 yards or meters. Choose which side seems most natural for you, but remember that you must breathe on the same side as the scissors kick.

**Success Goal** = kick 50 yards or meters of trudgen crawl kick on the side you choose to use and on which you will breathe

**Your Score** = (#) ____ yards or meters successfully kicked on your ____ side, which is now your chosen side

## 2. Trudgen Crawl Stroke Drill

Start in a prone float position. Goggles are optional. Begin a slow trudgen crawl kick sequence. On the second cycle, begin pulling and breathing on the same side as the scissors kick; add the second armstroke with the three flutter kicks. Do the stroke in slow motion, floating along at first, until you get the rhythm established between your arms and your legs. Then gradually increase the speed to a normal, easy trudgen crawl stroke. Remember, you *must* inhale on the scissors kick and exhale on the flutter kicks.

**Success Goal** = 100 yards or meters swimming trudgen crawl stroke easily and smoothly

**Your Score** = ____ maintained a smooth trudgen crawl stroke for the entire 100 yards or meters (yes or no?)

# Trudgen Strokes
# Keys to Success Checklists

The coordination of the trudgen stroke is so different from anything you have done that you need someone familiar with this stroke to rate you. Power should be evident in each double trudgen stroke. Use the checklists within Figures 14.1 and 14.2, respectively, to evaluate your progress.

# *Step 15* **Surface Dives**

Surface diving is diving under the water from a position on the surface. Three types of surface dives are mentioned by agencies that teach swimming classes: the pike surface dive, the tuck surface dive, and the feetfirst surface dive. Good watermanship requires that we learn all three.

## WHY ARE SURFACE DIVES IMPORTANT?

Surface dives are utilitarian skills, important tools that allow pleasure seekers and scuba divers to move more efficiently into the depths in pursuit of their goals. We may use surface dives for moving quickly and easily from the surface to a position underwater to recover objects, to swim under an obstruction, or to explore. In making a swimming rescue, an efficient surface dive may be very important indeed.

## HOW TO DO SURFACE DIVES

*CAUTION: Surface dives should not be learned in water less than 8 feet deep!* There is a danger of striking your head or toes on the bottom.

The three surface dives will be described here in this order: pike surface dive, tuck surface dive, and feetfirst surface dive. All three surface dives are illustrated in Figure 15.1.

### Pike Surface Dive

The pike surface dive is the choice of most persons. It is smooth and efficient, and it looks better than the others. Begin the pike surface dive from a prone float position with arms stretched overhead. Pull back with a wide sweep of both arms until your arms are at your sides. This should impart some forward momentum to your body. Turn your hands palm down as they finish the sweep.

Then keep both legs stretched and together, toes pointed, as you bend sharply at your waist (pike), driving your head and torso downward to a vertical position. Because of

your forward momentum, the water will press on your back as you bend, helping you keep your legs horizontal at the surface. Leave your hands palm down at your hips. Now press your arms downward against the water as you lift both straight legs, toes pointed, into a vertical position above you. The downward press of your arms provides the counteracting pressure to allow your legs to lift clear of the water. To avoid pressing you over onto your back, the press of your arms should stop when they point directly downward. Hold perfectly still in streamlined position to allow the weight of your lifted legs to drive you beneath the surface. As your toes go underwater, you may pull with both arms in a wide-sweeping breaststroke arm motion to pull you deeper or to level off for underwater swimming.

### Tuck Surface Dive

The tuck surface dive is a variation of the pike surface dive. Start from a prone position with arms stretched overhead. Sweep your arms outward and back to your sides and turn your hands palm down.

Then bend sharply 90 degrees at your waist, driving your head downward. As you then press downward with your arms, quickly tuck your knees to your chest and thrust them vertically upward, toes pointed, feet together. The weight of your legs will force you underwater. Do not press as hard or as long with your arms because with your body tucked, you will rotate more easily and your leg thrust may go past the vertical.

### Feetfirst Surface Dive

To do a feetfirst surface dive, assume a vertical, upright position in the water with your chin at water level. Position your legs for a powerful scissors kick and spread your arms to the side at the surface. Then kick and press simultaneously to lift your body as high as possible in the water. Your kick should finish with your legs together, and your arm press should finish with your arms tight against your sides. Leave them in this streamlined position as you rise and then sink, still upright, beneath the surface.

When your head is well under the water, turn your palms outward and lift strongly against the water to drive yourself deeper. Your hands should not break the surface on the arm lift. You may repeat the lift with your arms until you are as deep as you wish to go. Then proceed with your mission.

## Figure 15.1 Keys to Success: Surface Dives

### Pike and Tuck Dives

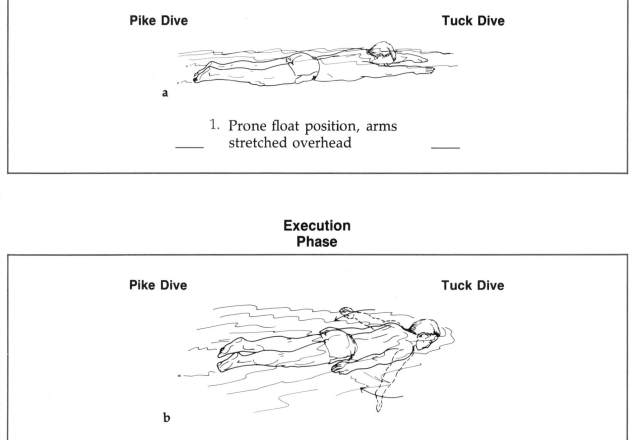

**Preparation Phase**

Pike Dive                                          Tuck Dive

a

1. Prone float position, arms stretched overhead

**Execution Phase**

Pike Dive                                          Tuck Dive

b

1. **Sweep:** Sweep both arms back to sides, turn palms down

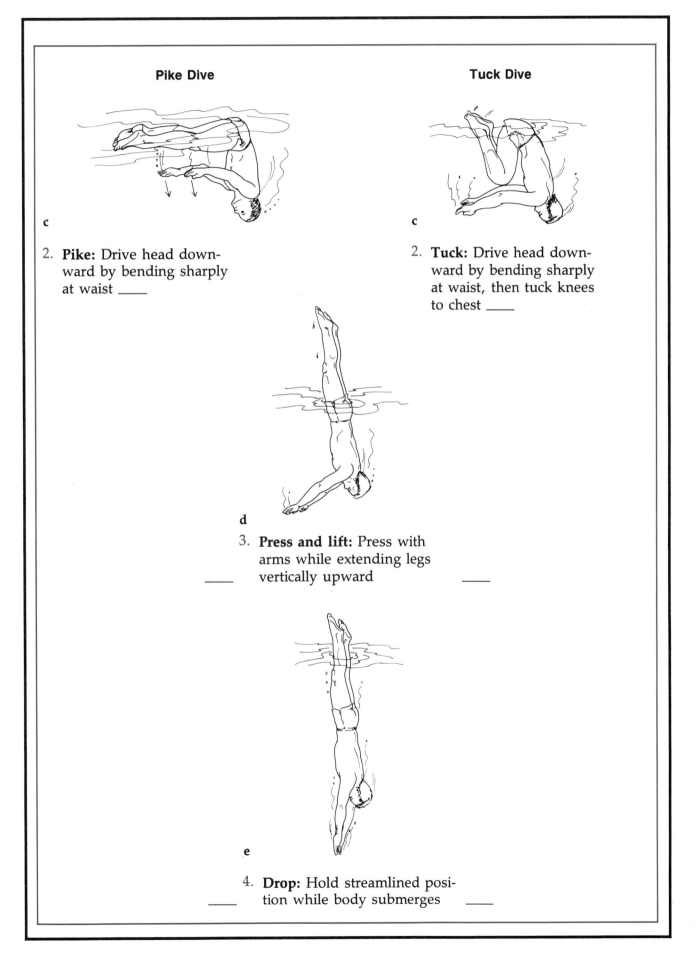

**Pike Dive**

c

2. **Pike:** Drive head downward by bending sharply at waist ____

**Tuck Dive**

c

2. **Tuck:** Drive head downward by bending sharply at waist, then tuck knees to chest ____

d

3. **Press and lift:** Press with arms while extending legs vertically upward

____                                           ____

e

4. **Drop:** Hold streamlined position while body submerges
____                                           ____

## Follow-Through
## Phase

| Pike Dive | | Tuck Dive |
|---|---|---|
| | 1. Level off for underwater swim, or return to surface ____ | |

## Feetfirst Dive

## Preparation
## Phase

1. Vertical position, chin at water level, arms out to sides, legs apart for scissors kick ____

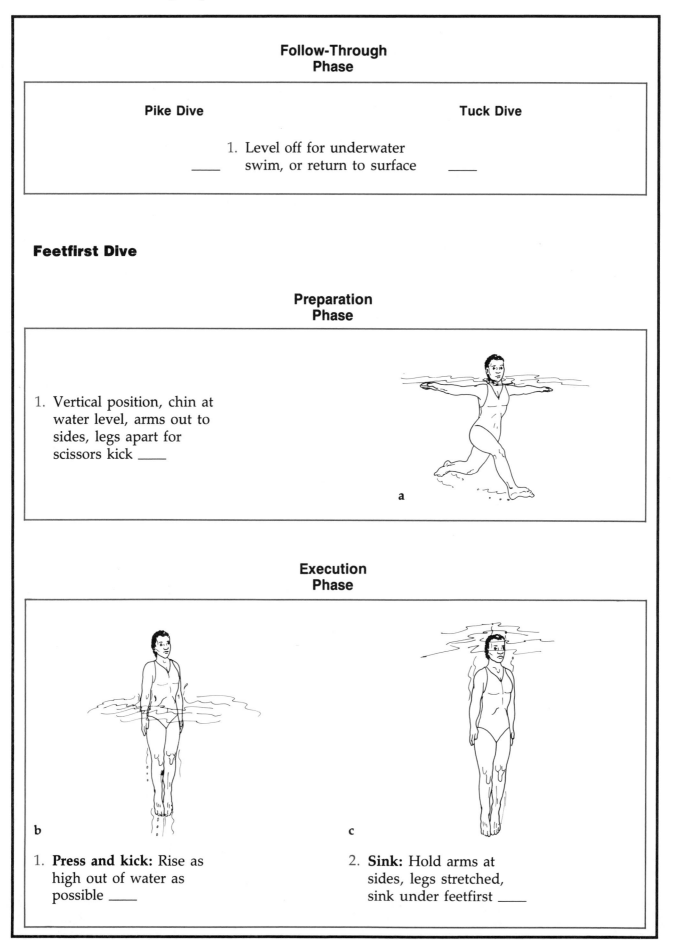

a

## Execution
## Phase

b

c

1. **Press and kick:** Rise as high out of water as possible ____

2. **Sink:** Hold arms at sides, legs stretched, sink under feetfirst ____

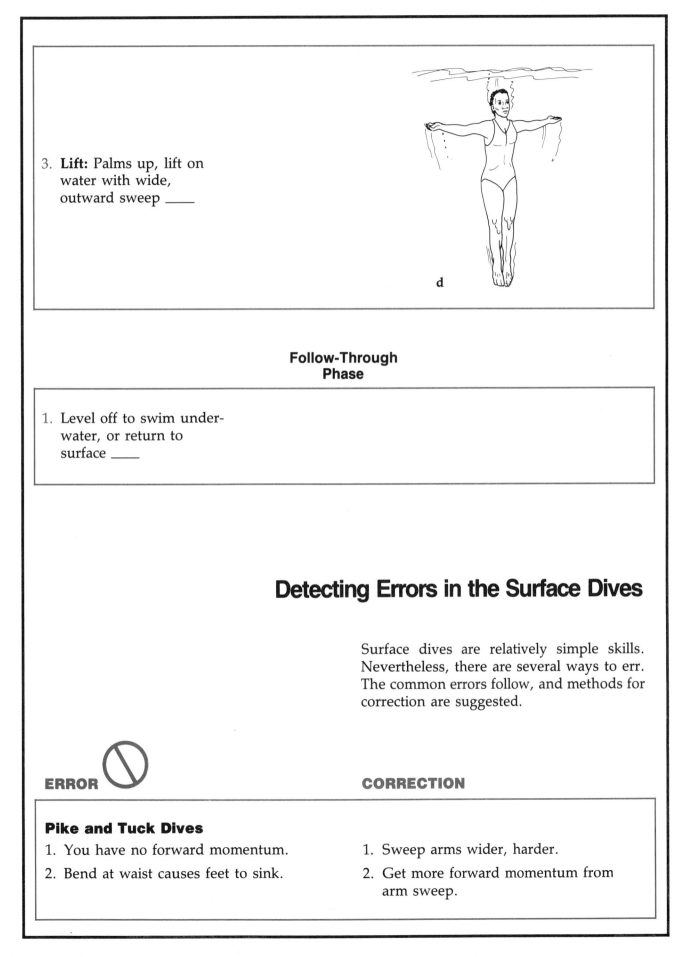

3. **Lift:** Palms up, lift on water with wide, outward sweep ____

d

**Follow-Through Phase**

1. Level off to swim under-water, or return to surface ____

# Detecting Errors in the Surface Dives

Surface dives are relatively simple skills. Nevertheless, there are several ways to err. The common errors follow, and methods for correction are suggested.

**ERROR**

**CORRECTION**

**Pike and Tuck Dives**

1. You have no forward momentum.

2. Bend at waist causes feet to sink.

1. Sweep arms wider, harder.

2. Get more forward momentum from arm sweep.

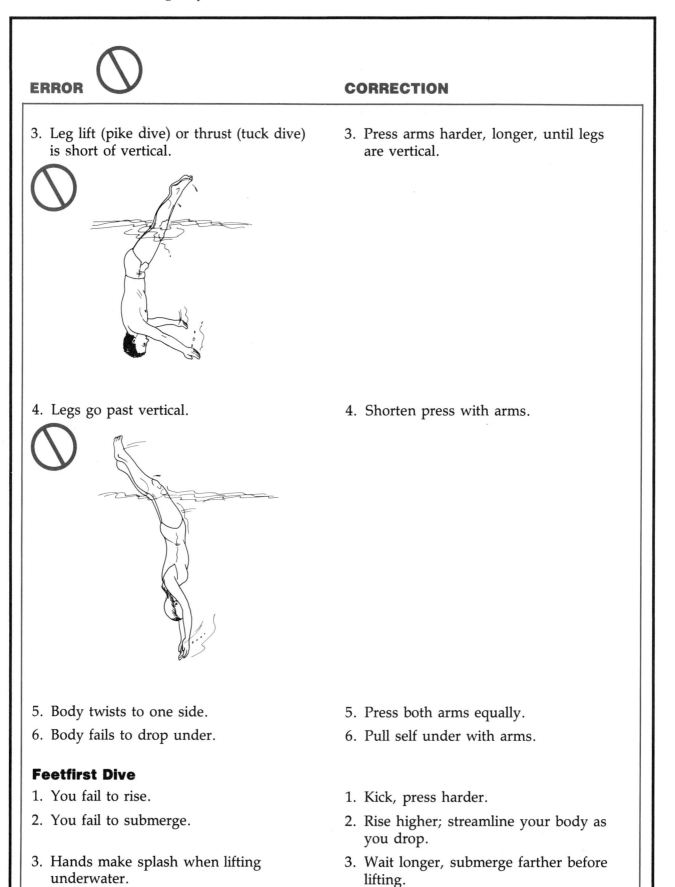

**ERROR**

**CORRECTION**

3. Leg lift (pike dive) or thrust (tuck dive) is short of vertical.

3. Press arms harder, longer, until legs are vertical.

4. Legs go past vertical.

4. Shorten press with arms.

5. Body twists to one side.

5. Press both arms equally.

6. Body fails to drop under.

6. Pull self under with arms.

**Feetfirst Dive**

1. You fail to rise.

1. Kick, press harder.

2. You fail to submerge.

2. Rise higher; streamline your body as you drop.

3. Hands make splash when lifting underwater.

3. Wait longer, submerge farther before lifting.

# Surface Dive Drills

CAUTION: *Learn all surface dives in water at least 8 feet deep!* Be careful not to strike your head or toes on the bottom.

## *1. Sweep and Pike Drill*

Wear goggles or mask and snorkel for this drill. In water at least 8 feet deep, assume a prone float position with arms stretched overhead. Take a deep breath and hold it. Sweep both arms out to the side and back just under the surface to start your body moving forward strongly. As you finish the sweep, leave your elbows straight and turn your palms to face the bottom of the pool.

Hold still in this position with hands at your hips as you pike sharply forward at your waist, forcing your head down until your body is bent at a right angle. Your goal is to achieve a position with your legs still near the surface, your head pointing directly at the bottom, and your hands still palms down beside your hips. *Freeze!* Hold this position for 5 seconds before coming up: Do not lift your legs above you, do not press downward with your arms. Hold the right-angle position rigidly for the 5 seconds.

**Success Goal** = 5 sweeps and pikes as described

**Your Score** = (#) _____ successful sweeps and pikes

## *2. Pike Without Sweep (Wrong Way)*

Try this drill just to impress upon yourself the importance of the sweep of the arms and the resulting forward momentum. In water at least 8 feet deep, assume a prone float position with your arms along your sides. With no preliminary motion, bend sharply at your waist, trying to drive your head and upper body to an inverted vertical position. Do not move your arms. Note that your upper body stops somewhat short of the vertical and that your legs and feet are quite deeply submerged.

**Success Goal** = realize that attaining a good preliminary surface dive position is very difficult without forward momentum

**Your Score** = _____ the extent to which you realize this

### 3. Leg Lift Without Arm Press (Wrong Way)

Try this drill to determine how important the arm press is for lifting your legs successfully. Assume the finishing position of Drill 2: body bent at a right angle, with head and trunk vertical under the water, legs horizontal at the surface, arms along sides, and hands at hips. Keep your arms motionless and try to lift your legs to a vertical position. You will discover that your legs hardly lift at all and your upper body rises to a nearly horizontal position.

**Success Goal** = realize that you cannot lift your legs into a vertical position without a counterbalancing downward press of your arms

**Your Score** = ____ the extent to which you realize this

### 4. Pike Surface Dive

*In water at least 8 feet deep*, wearing goggles or mask and snorkel, assume a prone float position with arms stretched overhead. Use the key words *sweep, bend, press and lift*, and *drop* to guide your actions.

Take a big breath and hold it. *Sweep* your arms wide at the surface until they are at your side; turn your palms to face the bottom. *Bend* sharply at your waist to drive your head and upper torso to a head-down vertical position, with hands still at your hips. *Press* downward strongly with both arms as you *lift* your straight legs behind you to a vertical position, stretched, together, and with toes pointed. Stop all motion when your legs attain a vertical position, allowing your body to *drop* gracefully beneath the surface. Then level off and return to the surface.

**Success Goal** = 5 perfectly beautiful, streamlined pike surface dives with legs straight and together and toes pointed

**Your Score** = (#) ____ really good dives

### 5. Tuck Surface Dive

*In water at least 8 feet deep*, wearing goggles or mask and snorkel, assume a prone float position with arms stretched overhead. Use the key words *sweep, bend, tuck, press and extend*, and *drop* to guide you.

Take a deep breath and hold it. *Sweep* your arms wide to your sides and turn your palms down. *Bend* sharply at your hips to a right angle with your head down and your legs horizontal. Immediately after bending, *tuck* your knees up to your chest, *press* your arms downward, and *extend* your legs to a vertical position. Keep your feet together and your toes pointed as you *drop* beneath the surface. Pull with your arms to level off, then return to the surface.

**Success Goal =** 5 streamlined, vertical tuck surface dives with feet together, legs straight, and toes pointed

**Your Score =** (#) ___ good dives

## 6. Feetfirst Surface Dive

Wear goggles for this drill. In water more than 8 feet deep, scull and kick to maintain a vertical position with your chin at water level. Take a deep breath and hold it. Extend both arms out to the sides as far as you can reach on the surface; step forward and back in preparation for a large, powerful scissors kick. Kick powerfully and press on the water with both arms to lift yourself as high as possible out of the water. As your legs finish the kick and your arms finish the press, keep your legs together, toes pointed, and your arms pressed to your sides as you submerge.

When your head is about 8 to 12 inches underwater, turn your palms outward and lift outward with your arms strongly to force yourself deeper underwater. *Be careful not to drive your pointed toes into the bottom.* Tuck your knees, turn to a level position, and swim forward and upward to the surface.

**Success Goal =** 5 consecutive feetfirst surface dives with no splash upon submerging and to a depth of at least 5 feet when you level off

**Your Score =** (#) ___ successful dives

# Surface Dives
# Keys to Success Checklist

Numbers of surface dives completed is meaningless unless the dives were properly done. Good surface dives have an aesthetic appearance that cannot be measured objectively.

Have your instructor or a knowledgeable friend rate your performance according to the checklists within Figure 15.1.

# *Step 16* Underwater Swimming

Swimming underwater is fun, safe when properly regulated, and very useful, but there are inherent dangers to consider. It is rather obvious that unless you are using underwater breathing apparatus, you must hold your breath while swimming underwater. Perhaps the most important aspect of swimming underwater is learning to set limits on your breath-holding to prevent loss of consciousness and, probably, your life. Please read the "Be Safe" section of this step very carefully.

## WHY IS SWIMMING UNDERWATER IMPORTANT?

Rescue of submerged victims is very important. Recovery of submerged objects may be very important. Underwater swimming is a means for accomplishing such rescue and recovery. It is also much fun for exploration, and it is important that watermanship skills should be developed for enjoyment as well as for useful purposes.

## BE SAFE

Swimming underwater is subject to two inherent dangers: limited visibility, and a physiological phenomenon called "underwater blackout," which is due to prolonged breath-holding.

### Limited Visibility

Wearing goggles or a mask when swimming underwater greatly helps decrease the danger of underwater swimming. However, the clarity of the water cannot always be controlled, so special precautions are necessary when turbid water restricts visibility. It could ruin your whole day to pull strongly with both arms in water of zero visibility and thrust your head into a battleship you didn't see. In turbid water always take short pulling strokes (within your range of visibility) and glide with arms in front of you.

### Hyperventilation

Unfortunately, too many persons are employing hyperventilation to increase their breath-holding ability. This technique consists of breathing deeply and rapidly for 10 or 20 breaths or more and then trying to hold one's breath or swim underwater for as long as possible.

For physiological reasons, the practice of hyperventilation is very dangerous. Air taken into the lungs provides the oxygen the body requires to function. Blood carries the oxygen from the lungs to the brain, muscles, and every other part of the body. When muscles use oxygen, they form carbon dioxide, which is carried away from the muscle by the blood flow. Thus, as oxygen is depleted, there is a corresponding increase in the carbon dioxide content of the blood. The body does not measure the decrease in oxygen but reacts to the increase in carbon dioxide by signaling the breathing center in the brain to take in more air.

It is a common belief that hyperventilation increases the oxygen content of the blood and allows a person to hold his or her breath longer. Hyperventilation does not significantly increase the oxygen content of the blood, but it does tend to purge the bloodstream of carbon dioxide, thus depriving the body of its defensive mechanism that tells the breathing center to cause more breathing. If the bloodstream is purged of its normal carbon dioxide content, it will take longer to generate the signal to breathe. The body is fooled into thinking it does not need to take in more air, when in fact the oxygen supply could be seriously depleted.

The result of this phenomenon is that a person may feel perfectly comfortable holding his or her breath and may not feel a need to breathe before the oxygen supply to the brain is depleted and the person loses consciousness. Despite unconsciousness, the carbon dioxide level would eventually build to the point of triggering the breathing mechanism. The person would inhale involuntarily, even if underwater.

*Never, never try to extend your breath-holding time by hyperventilation before swimming underwater.* No possible reason for underwater swimming could warrant the risk.

## HOW TO SWIM UNDERWATER

The distance you can swim underwater is governed by the efficiency of your stroke and how long you can hold your breath. The efficiency of your stroke depends upon the exact technical excellence of your propulsive movements, the maximum use of streamlining techniques to reduce drag, and relaxing your muscles to the maximum extent consistent with maintaining propulsive movements and streamlining. A relaxed muscle uses oxygen less rapidly than a tense one.

The most powerful swimming arm motion we know is the butterfly armstroke. The most powerful kick we know is either the scissors kick or the breaststroke kick, depending on which you do better. By combining these propulsive factors with a long, relaxed glide, we can swim underwater most efficiently.

In clear water with good visibility, wear goggles or a mask, take a big breath, do a surface dive, and level off. Start underwater in a horizontal position with arms overhead and body streamlined. Pull back and slightly upward with a long, powerful butterfly armstroke. Streamline your body for a glide with arms tight to your sides. Your body will tend to rise as you glide because of your buoyancy.

Therefore, you must maintain a slightly head-down position and pull slightly upward on each stroke, as if you were swimming downhill. While gliding, relax as much as possible while still maintaining a streamlined position.

Continue to glide until your forward motion nearly, but not quite, stops. Then, keeping your hands close to your body to minimize drag, bring them under your stomach to chest level as you recover your legs into position for a scissors or breaststroke kick (whichever you do better). Kick immediately and powerfully as you thrust your hands, fingertips first, into full extension. Glide again in relaxed and streamlined position until your forward motion nearly stops. Continue this cycle of pull, glide, kick, glide as long as you can hold your breath without undue stress. Then return to the surface.

During your glide it is important to relax your stomach muscles consciously. Most swimmers maintain very tense abdominal muscles during underwater swimming, which uses oxygen very rapidly. Some swimmers feel that exhaling a very small amount relieves them of distress. However, any exhalation reduces the amount of oxygen available to you. It is best to retain all of your air while swimming underwater.

In water of poor visibility, do not glide with your arms at your sides. Make sure you can see two body lengths ahead, then pull through, but recover your arms and kick immediately into full arm extension before gliding. The poor-visibility stroke for underwater swimming has the same coordination as the breaststroke: pull, recover to chest, kick, arms forward, glide.

# Detecting Errors in Underwater Swimming

Efficiency in underwater swimming depends upon disciplined movements. There are some common errors that rob your stroke of efficiency. Try to recognize and correct your errors with the help of the following list.

**ERROR** 🚫                                 **CORRECTION**

| ERROR | CORRECTION |
|---|---|
| 1. You exhale while swimming. | 1. Hold all your air. |
| 2. You float to surface. | 2. Pull your arms back and upward, swimming "downhill." |
| 3. You stroke constantly. | 3. Glide after each pull and each kick. |
| 4. You prolong leg recovery. | 4. Recover your legs quickly and kick immediately. |
| 5. You use flutter kick. | 5. Use a large, strong kick, which uses oxygen more slowly. |
| 6. You glide headfirst in murky water. | 6. No, no! Battleships may be lurking about! Keep your arms in front of your head. |

# Underwater Swimming Drills

## 1. Underwater Glide for Distance

Wear goggles or a mask. Stand in 4 feet of water at the pool edge, with your back to the wall. Take two deep breaths, hold the second one, and sink beneath the surface. Place both feet against the wall behind you, extend both arms ahead, and hook your thumbs. Push off, streamline—keeping your head between your arms and pointing your toes—and hold perfectly still. You will float to the surface. Continue to hold your breath as long as you can, even if it seems that you have stopped moving. When you must breathe, stop. Note or mark the distance you glided.

    Try again from the same starting point, but pay more attention to maintaining a totally streamlined position. Consciously relax your stomach muscles while gliding. How far can you glide?

**Success Goal** = 45 feet of glide

**Your Score** = (#) _____ feet; try again!

## 2. Underwater Swimming Stroke Coordination

Use a mask and a snorkel for this drill. Float in a prone position, breathing through the snorkel. Stretch both arms overhead. Perform a long, full butterfly pull but stop when your hands reach your thighs. Streamline and glide for a count of 3 (approximately 3 seconds). Keep your hands close to your body and bring them forward under your chest to your chin.

As your hands are recovering, bring your legs into position for either a breaststroke kick or a scissors kick, whichever you do better. If you choose a scissors kick, it will be necessary to twist your hips to the side somewhat to keep your feet underwater. When your legs are positioned, kick vigorously and drive your arms forward to full extension. Glide for a count of 3 and start the next stroke. Thus, your key timing words will be *pull, glide, kick, glide; pull, glide, kick, glide*; and so on.

**Success Goal** = 25 yards or meters of underwater swimming stroke with steady rhythm

**Your Score** = (#) _____ yards or meters

## 3. Underwater Swimming From a Surface Dive

Do this drill in clear water more than 8 feet deep. Wear goggles or a mask and a snorkel. Take two deep breaths, hold the second one, and do a surface dive, leveling off at a depth of about 6 feet. Immediately begin swimming underwater. To maintain your depth against the lift of buoyancy, assume a slightly head-down position and be sure to pull up somewhat on the water at the beginning of each pull. If the water is not too deep, it is helpful to follow the contour of the pool bottom to judge your depth.

*Do not force yourself to hold your breath beyond normal comfort limits!*

**Success Goal** = ability to maintain constant depth and rhythm for whatever distance you cover

**Your Score** = _____ maintained a steady depth and stroke rhythm (yes or no?)

## 4. Murky Water Swimming Stroke on Surface

On the surface, with mask and snorkel, begin in prone float position with arms stretched overhead, breathing through your snorkel. Pull with a long, powerful butterfly stroke. Immediately initiate recovery of arms and legs and kick into extended glide position. Glide only when your arms are extended overhead to protect your head from unseen obstacles. Your key words are *pull, kick, glide*.

**Success Goal** = 25 yards or meters in correct pull-and-kick rhythm

**Your Score** = (#) _____ yards or meters

## 5. Murky Water Stroke Underwater

Do this drill in *clear* water more than 8 feet deep, wearing goggles or mask and snorkel. Take two deep breaths, hold the second one, and do a surface dive. Level off at a depth of about 6 feet and immediately begin using the murky water stroke for swimming underwater (Drill 4). Do not glide with hands at your sides; glide only when your arms are forward. The rhythm is nearly the same as for breaststroke, except that the pull is much longer.

*Do not force yourself to hold your breath beyond normal comfort limits!* Concentrate on the stroke, not the distance.

**Success Goal** = ability to maintain constant depth and stroke rhythm for whatever distance you swim

**Your Score** = ____ maintained constant depth and proper rhythm (yes or no?)

# Step 17   Universal Sculling

Sculling is using your hands to apply constant, unvarying pressure on the water, perpendicular to the direction in which your hands are moving. Your hands, moving in a horizontal plane, can apply pressure vertically downward—or upward.

Universal sculling is a term coined for the application of sculling to a myriad of skills and stunts. I sincerely hope that you will experiment beyond the descriptions in this text to develop new applications for sculling to further prove its universality.

## WHY IS UNIVERSAL SCULLING IMPORTANT?

Perhaps no other skill in aquatics is more important than sculling. It transcends the sport of swimming and is a basic skill for any aquatic sport that requires participants to enter the water. Sculling is a fundamental part of most swimming strokes. It is the basis on which all synchronized swimming is built. Lifesaving and nearly all water safety skills employ sculling. Water polo players scull constantly. Is sculling important? You can bet your life on it!

## HOW TO DO UNIVERSAL SCULLING

How do you do universal sculling? Any way you want to! I will describe the fundamentals, give you some drills that will polish your skill, and challenge you to create new uses.

I'll start by describing sculling as it is used to support your body in the water; this works by moving your hands in a horizontal plane to apply downward pressure. Stand in water of chin depth. Extend your arms in front of you, with your hands 6 inches under the water, elbows bent nearly 90 degrees. Hold your hands flat, palms down, and about 3 feet apart. Keep your wrists straight but twist your forearms so your palms face partially inward at angles about 45 degrees to the horizontal. If you were to try to move your hands inward toward each other, holding them at that angle,

they would tend to rise to follow the line of least resistance toward the edge of your hand. If you make them move inward in an exactly horizontal plane, though, you will have to apply downward pressure to keep them from rising. Your hands will move horizontally, but you are applying force in a vertical, downward direction. That force, transmitted through your arms to your body, will support you in the water.

Because of its angle of 45 degrees, your right hand is applying force not only partially downward but also partially inward. This inward force on the right hand tends to move you to the right, but your left hand is applying an equal force tending to move you to the left, so the two forces cancel each other. The resultant force is downward only.

Continue to move your hands inward until they are almost touching. When they stop moving, they stop applying downward force. Now quickly rotate your hands and forearms so your hands face outward at 45-degree angles. Immediately start to move them apart. Now the force on your right hand is downward and outward. The downward force tends to support you, again, and the outward force tends to move you to the left. However, your left hand is also applying an outward force that cancels out the right hand's outward push; once again the residual force is a supporting downward force. By continually moving your hands inward and outward on a horizontal plane, you can support yourself to keep your head above the water.

At each extreme of your sculling motion, while you are in the process of rotating your hands, you are applying no downward force, leaving a dead spot, so to speak. However, if you press directly downward on the water during the time you rotate your hands, you can maintain a downward pressure even then. Your hands are now lower in the water than before, and you cannot continue to press them deeper at each end of the sculling motion.

Solve this problem by sculling slightly uphill. Scull inward and slightly up until your hands are nearly touching. Then press down as you rotate your arms. Scull outward and slightly upward to the outer end of your sculling motion, then press downward again and repeat the process. The result is a figure 8 motion of your hands (see Figure 17.1). A steady, unvarying pressure is thus maintained throughout the sculling. Sculling for support without moving through the water is called ''a neutral scull'' or ''sculling in place.''

## *Figure 17.1 Keys to Success: Universal Sculling*

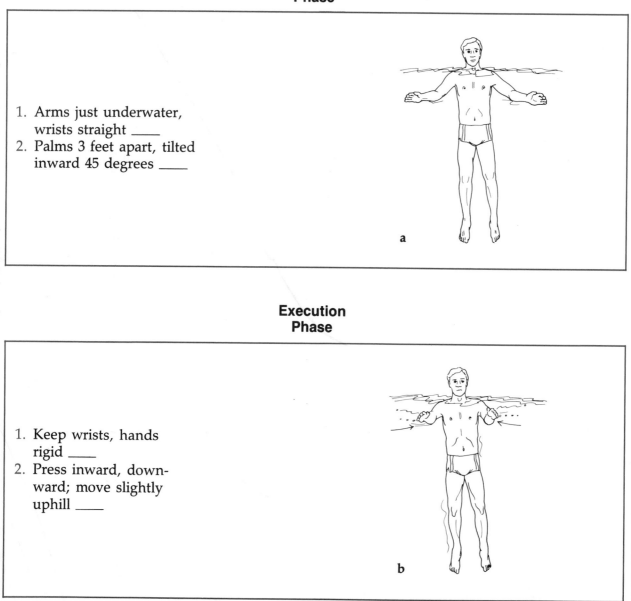

**Preparation Phase**

1. Arms just underwater, wrists straight ____
2. Palms 3 feet apart, tilted inward 45 degrees ____

a

**Execution Phase**

1. Keep wrists, hands rigid ____
2. Press inward, downward; move slightly uphill ____

b

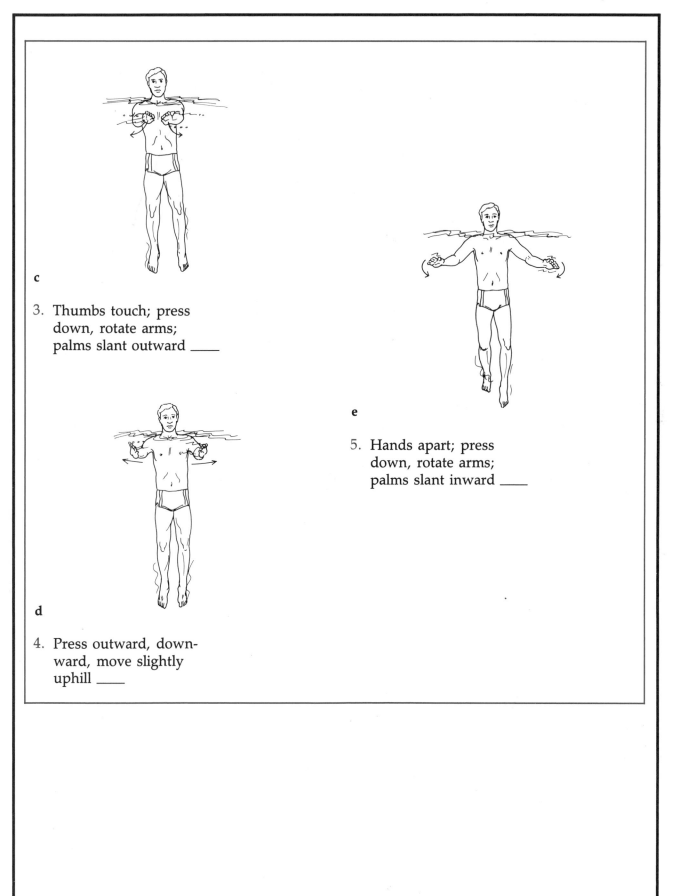

c

3. Thumbs touch; press down, rotate arms; palms slant outward ____

d

4. Press outward, downward, move slightly uphill ____

e

5. Hands apart; press down, rotate arms; palms slant inward ____

### Follow-Through Phase

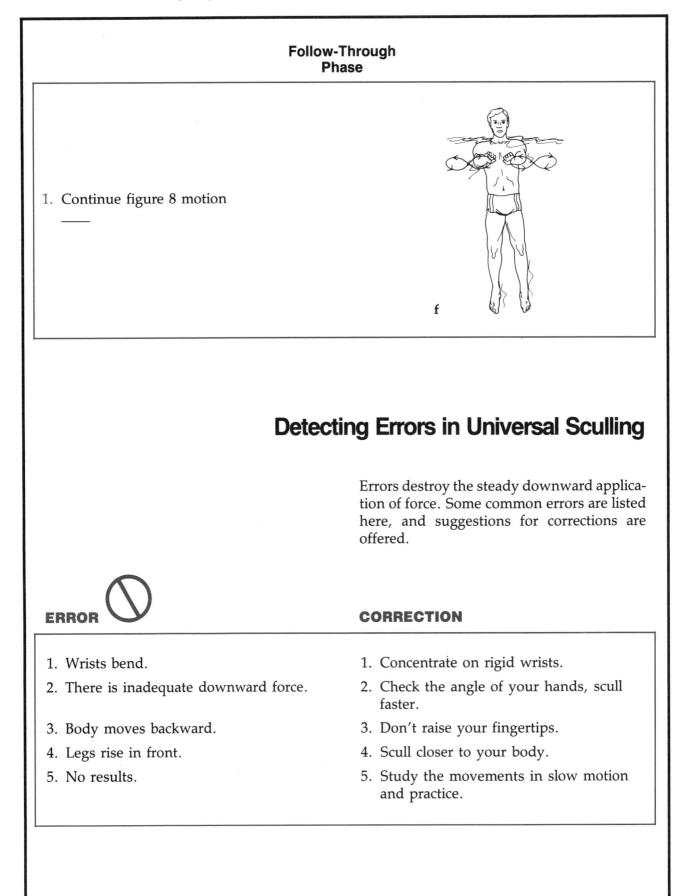

1. Continue figure 8 motion
   ——

f

## Detecting Errors in Universal Sculling

Errors destroy the steady downward application of force. Some common errors are listed here, and suggestions for corrections are offered.

| ERROR | CORRECTION |
|---|---|
| 1. Wrists bend. | 1. Concentrate on rigid wrists. |
| 2. There is inadequate downward force. | 2. Check the angle of your hands, scull faster. |
| 3. Body moves backward. | 3. Don't raise your fingertips. |
| 4. Legs rise in front. | 4. Scull closer to your body. |
| 5. No results. | 5. Study the movements in slow motion and practice. |

# Universal Sculling Drills

## 1. Neutral Scull

Stand in chin-deep water. Extend your hands in front, 30 to 36 inches apart and 6 to 8 inches underwater, with elbows bent, wrists straight, and hands tilted 45 degrees inward. Press downward and inward to bring your hands together in a nearly horizontal plane, allowing them to rise slightly. Press directly down as you rotate your forearms to turn your palms outward at 45-degree angles. Press downward and outward in a nearly horizontal plane, allowing your hands to rise slightly, until they are 30 to 36 inches apart. Once again press directly downward as you rotate your forearms again to bring your hands to positions facing inward at 45 degrees.

Continue this figure 8 motion, pressing on the water hard enough to maintain your position as you lift your feet from the bottom (a). Continue the sculling motion as you extend your elbows and scull farther in front of you. As your elbows straighten, the rotating motion to maintain the 45-degree hand slant will become a rotating motion from your shoulders. Your entire arm will rotate to turn your hands. Keep your wrists rigid and perfectly straight.

Allow your feet to rise, straighten your hips, and lie back. As your feet come to the surface, you will be sculling at your hips on either side of your body (b). Continue to scull until your hips and your feet are at the top of the water. Drop your fingertips slightly (by bending your wrists, not your knuckles) to negate any head-first motion of your body.

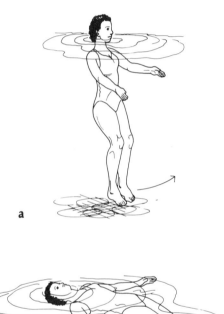

a

b

### Success Goal =

bring your body from vertical to horizontal and maintain your hips and your feet at the surface for 2 minutes

### Your Score =

(#) _____ minutes with hips and feet at surface

## 2. Neutral Scull on Back

Start in a back float position with your toes just 2 inches from the pool edge. Scull at your hips to maintain your hips and your feet at the surface and to keep your toes within 6 inches of the wall.

If your feet move out from the wall, it is because your wrists are bending slightly back and your fingertips are rising slightly. Flex your wrists forward to lower your fingertips as you scull. If you dig your fingertips in too deeply, you will move toward your feet. Practice until you can hold your position without moving toward either your head or your feet.

**Success Goal =** maintain your horizontal position for 2 minutes without either feetfirst or headfirst motion

**Your Score =** (#) _____ minutes of sculling in place

## 3. Sculling Headfirst on Your Back

Start in a back float position, sculling at your hips to maintain position. Gradually bend your wrists back until your fingertips are pointing upward at about 45 degrees. Continue to scull, rotating your arms from your shoulders so that the heels of your hands move alternately inward (a) and outward (b), leading the fingertips. Maintain downward pressure, also, so your hips and feet remain at the surface. You will move headfirst.

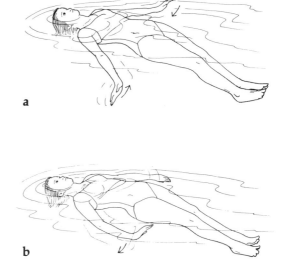

**Success Goal =**

45 feet of sculling headfirst with hips and feet up

**Your Score =**

(#) _____ feet of sculling headfirst

## 4. Feetfirst Sculling on Your Back

Start in a back float position with your head toward the pool edge. Scull in position (neutral scull) until your hips and your feet are at the surface. Then gradually flex your wrists forward so your fingertips point deeper toward the bottom of the pool. Keep your elbows locked straight and continue to scull, rotating your entire arms from the shoulders so your fingertips lead alternately inward and outward from your hips. Maintain downward pressure to keep your hips and your feet up, but pull yourself forward with your fingertips as you scull.

**Success Goal =** 45 feet sculling feetfirst with hips and feet at the surface

**Your Score =**

(#) ___ feet of sculling feetfirst in good position

## 5. Sculling Pivot

Start in a back float position doing a neutral scull (sculling in place). Flex one wrist forward, pointing fingertips down; bend the other wrist back, pointing fingertips up. Continue sculling. Keep your body rigidly straight. The hand pointing down will pull on that side; the hand pointing up will push on that side. The result should be that your body will pivot as though it were turning on a post at your hips. You should not move in a circle but should pivot in place. Reverse your hand positions to pivot in the other direction.

**Success Goal =** pivot 360 degrees in place in each direction

**Your Score =** (#) ___ pivots in each direction

## 6. Circle Sculling on Your Back

Start from a neutral scull on your back, sculling at your hips. Keep one wrist absolutely straight, the hand twisting by shoulder rotation. Bend your other wrist back to elevate the fingertips. Continue to scull. The elevated fingertips should propel that side of your body headfirst, causing you to move in a large circle. Reverse the hand positions to reverse the direction of the circle. You can use the backstroke turn flags as a centerline to guide your course.

**Success Goal =**

scull in a complete figure 8 on your back with hips and feet at the surface

**Your Score =**

(#) ___ figure 8s completed

## 7. Canoe Scull

"Canoe" is simply a name given to sculling in this position. To do this drill, start in a prone float position. Keeping your elbows in close to your sides, bend them so your hands are pointing at the bottom of the pool. Bend your wrists back so your palms are facing partly toward your feet and partly toward the bottom of the pool. Begin sculling, leading with the heels of your hands and moving your hands alternately in and out from your body. Scull near your hips, under your body. Rotate your forearms to change the direction of your palms. Your elbows will move out from your body to lead the hands away, then will lead your hands in again.

You should be able to apply enough force downward on the water so that you can lift your head forward and hold it up with your chin at water level for breathing. By arching your back strongly, you will keep the heels of your feet at the surface. You will also be applying force backward on the water, which should move you forward, as well.

**Success Goal =**

hold good canoe position for 20 to 25 feet

**Your Score =**

(#) _____ feet in good canoe position

## 8. Overhead Scull, Headfirst, Prone Position

Start in a prone float position with both arms stretched overhead. Flex your wrists forward to point your fingertips at the bottom of the pool. Keep your elbows rigidly straight and rotate your arms from the shoulders to point your fingertips alternately inward and outward. Leading with your fingertips, pull outward about 12 to 18 inches. Then rotate the fingertips inward and let them lead as you pull inward again. This sculling motion will feel as if you are pulling your body along by your fingertips (you are!). Scull forward, lifting your chin for a breath, then dropping your face into the water again.

**Success Goal =**

   15 feet of headfirst motion, sculling overhead in a prone position

**Your Score =**

   (#) ____ feet of sculling overhead in prone position

## 9. Torpedo Scull

Do the following short land drill first. Stand erect with both arms over your head. Imagine that the ceiling is just within reach of your hands. Bend your wrists back to place your palms flat ''against'' the ceiling. Now move your arms and hands alternately apart and together sideways, leading with the heels of your hands. Thus ''polish the ceiling.'' Allow your elbows to bend to reach somewhat behind you. Continue, first with heels leading out, then with twist from shoulder, heels leading in, twist again, and so on.

Now put on a nose clip, take a back float position in the water, and ''polish the ceiling'' beyond your head. Take and hold as much air as you can to give you maximum buoyancy. You should move feetfirst rather rapidly. To keep your feet from sinking, tighten your stomach muscles to eliminate the arch in your back, bend very slightly at the hips to raise your legs a little, and point your toes until the bottoms of your feet are slanted 45 degrees upward. The faster you go, the better your feet and legs will plane upward to stay at the surface.

If you don't bend your wrists back far enough, they will face partly toward the surface of the water, causing an upward push that will sink your head. Bend your wrists back farther—and even bend your elbows more, if necessary—to make your palms face directly overhead.

**Success Goal =**

30 feet, feetfirst like a torpedo in the water

**Your Score =**

(#) _____ feet of torpedo scull

## 10. Sculling Sideways

When doing a neutral scull, your hands are slanted alternately outward and inward. The slant positions apply both outward and inward pushes against the water. Because the outward push of the right hand exactly counteracts the outward push of the left hand, no sideways movement is possible—or is it? Suppose one hand were slanted more than the other. Then the forces would be unequal, and sideways motion would result.

Stand in the shallow end of the pool and place both hands and forearms flat on the pool deck, palms down (if your pool doesn't lend itself to this, get out of the water and use a table). Move your hands apart about 2 feet. Now carefully slant your left hand, thumb upwards, about 10 degrees from the horizontal (still nearly flat). Slant your right hand, thumb up, about 80 degrees from the horizontal (almost perpendicular). Now move them slowly together (a). You can see that the right hand would have more pull on the water than the left; this would tend to move you to the right. When your hands are close, reverse the slant. This time the left hand will slant about 80 degrees, palm out, and the right hand will slant about 10 degrees, little finger high. Now move them apart (b). The left hand will push harder than the right, causing you once again to move to the right. Continue to scull, carefully varying the hand tilt as before. Remember that the flat hand cannot be perfectly flat and the steep hand cannot be perfectly upright, or all downward pressure would be lost and no supporting force would remain.

Now take a back floating position in the water, hands at your hips, and do a neutral scull. Slowly begin to change the tilt of your hands until you are pushing and pulling more to one side than the other. *Voila!* The "impossible" sideways movement occurs.

a

b

**Success Goal =**

toes remain 6 inches from the pool wall
as you scull sideways 10 feet in each
direction

**Your Score =**

(#) ____ feet sculled to the right
(#) ____ feet sculled to the left

## 11. The Ultimate Test

You can now scull headfirst, feetfirst, and sideways. You can turn, pivot, and do a canoe scull on your stomach. Can you put them together?

Take a back float position at one corner of the pool. Your objective is to move diagonally across the pool from one corner to the far corner. You are to keep your body perfectly rigid, your feet together, and your toes pointed the whole time. Start moving forward and sideways and begin to pivot as you go, always moving along the diagonal line. Then add a roll from your back to canoe scull on your stomach; roll again to return onto your back, all the while sculling forward and sideways, or feetfirst and sideways, along the diagonal line.

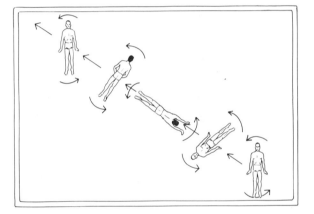

**Success Goal =**

smooth, straight line while pivoting and
rolling

**Your Score =**

____ maintained a smooth, straight line
while pivoting and rolling (yes or no?)

# Universal Sculling
# Keys to Success Checklist

Aesthetic evaluation is more than usually important in sculling. The opinion of a teacher or a coach is vital to your progress. Have someone knowledgeable evaluate your skill using the checklist in Figure 17.1.

## *Step 18* **Challenges in Watermanship**

We are weightless in water. We can therefore perform feats of physical prowess unattainable on land. We can, with some diligent application, combine parts of various swimming strokes to create new, interesting, and challenging strokes. This step challenges you to do just that: create new strokes, stunts, and games.

### WHY ARE STROKE CHALLENGES IN WATERMANSHIP IMPORTANT?

It is very important to have fun in the water, and the following new strokes are fun to try. It is also important to try new combinations of skills—to experiment—for research of this kind leads to the development of new, practical aquatic skills. Challenges are also important to competitive swimmers because some of these strokes are now finding their way into competition at the national championship level. Why don't you become famous by inventing a new and even faster stroke? It could be named after you!

### Dolphin Crawl Stroke

This stroke has actually been used in competition. One highly ranked swimmer used this stroke to produce a burst of speed during the last lap of a middle-distance race. It worked!

In prone float position, start a slow, rhythmic dolphin kick in sets of two. After the second set of two kicks, add a one-armed butterfly arm pull to the next set of two kicks. Then pull with your opposite arm on the next set of two kicks. Turn your head to the side and inhale during the pull of one arm. Turn your face down and exhale during the pull of your other arm.

Continue pulling with alternate armstrokes to the butterfly stroke rhythm. Smooth out the timing so your legs are kicking a constant 4-beat rhythm: down, up, down, up. Now begin to feel that it is not a butterfly stroke you

are swimming but a crawl stroke instead, with two dolphin kicks accompanying each armstroke.

### Dolphin Back Crawl Stroke

After learning the dolphin crawl stroke, the next logical step would be to learn the dolphin back crawl stroke. In a recent national championship swimming meet, some of the contestants in the backstroke event pushed off the wall on their backs and kicked almost a pool length underwater using the inverted dolphin kick. They did not use their arms with the dolphin kick, but it may have been a start toward introducing the dolphin kick into the back crawl stroke.

Start with a back glide, arms stretched overhead. Do an inverted dolphin kick, undulating from your hips and emphasizing the upward lifting of your feet and lower legs. Kick in pairs of upward beats, counting as for the prone dolphin kick: 1, and, 2, a-a-n-d. Do the two upward beats as a pair, then slow the downward recovery of your legs on the slow "a-a-n-d" count. Then pull through a back crawl armstroke on the next pair of upward kicks, getting your arm all the way through the pull on Counts 1 and "and"; return it to the water overhead on Count 2. Rest both arms overhead for the longer "a-a-n-d" count. This is exactly the same coordination as for the butterfly stroke, except that it involves only one arm.

On the next set of two kicks, pull through with the opposite arm, returning it to the water overhead on the count of 2, also. Rest both arms again for the long "a-a-n-d."

Repeat, alternating arm pulls with each set of two kicks, but don't forget to pause for a slow count as your feet drop deeper in readiness for another two upward-thrust beats. Inhale during an arm pull; exhale during the pull of the opposite arm. Try to pull exactly as in the back crawl stroke, bending your elbow during the pull and recovering your arm straight and vertically. Slow down the kick rhythm so you don't have to pull so fast. Again, *slow down!*

### Butterfly Backstroke

Rules for swimming backstroke in competition say only that you must stay on your back for the entire race. You may move your arms and legs in any pattern you wish. It is even legal to swim the stroke using a double overarm recovery if you wish—especially so if you win!

Start in a back glide position with arms stretched overhead. Begin an inverted dolphin kick in paired kicks, as for the butterfly stroke. Just before kicking upward to begin the second set of kicks, pull both arms in a wide, sweeping pull just under the surface and toward your feet. Bend your elbows slightly to keep your hands a little closer to you. Kick upward with the dolphin kick as your arms reach midpull. Count 1 comes as you kick. Finish the arm pull all the way to your thighs and immediately lift both straight arms over the water as you drop your feet on the ''and'' count of the kick. Kick upward again (Count 2) as your arms enter the water stretched fully overhead. Rest your arms in glide position during a longer ''a-a-n-d'' count, while you drop your feet in preparation for the next stroke. You have completed one stroke.

Keep the coordination for this stroke exactly as for the butterfly stroke. Pull on Count 1, then hit the water with your arms on Count 2 for a glide. Be sure your arms glide for a long count between strokes. Keep your arms straight for the recovery over water and bend them slightly during the pull. Do not try to pull deep; your arms should pull horizontally about 6 inches underwater. Inhale during the pull, and exhale during the glide.

### Butterfly Breaststroke

The term *butterfly* refers to an arm motion. A butterfly breaststroke, then, would be a breaststroke with a butterfly arm motion. The butterfly breaststroke was an important evolutionary discovery in the 1940s. It was developed in a search for greater speed in the breaststroke by eliminating the underwater resistance of the arm recovery. The competitive swimming rules at the time did not anticipate such a move and, so, did not prohibit an over-the-water recovery. The kick and the timing remained the same, but the new overarm recovery broke all existing records, and its peculiar appearance was the origin of the term *butterfly* in swimming.

Begin from a prone glide position, arms stretched overhead. Recover your legs for a breaststroke kick, then kick as you pull through a butterfly arm pull. At the very end of the pull of your arms, recover your legs quickly; kick a second time as your arms recover over the water. Use a standard breaststroke kick. Glide while your legs recover, then repeat the action. Inhale during the pull of your arms; exhale during the glide.

## WHY ARE FUN CHALLENGES IN WATERMANSHIP IMPORTANT?

There are many, many fun things to do in the aquatic habitat. Here are a few more examples to get you started; then you can invent as many as your heart desires. Let your imagination run wild! Try things that are impossible on land but are great fun in the wonderful world of water.

### Marlin Turn

The marlin turn is a basic movement in synchronized swimming. It is easy and fun to do. It does not move you through the water, but it changes your position by exactly 90 degrees in relation to the pool edges. The marlin turn opens a new area of watermanship on which we touched only briefly in the step on universal sculling (Step 17).

The marlin turn starts with a horizontal back float parallel to the pool edge; from this position you do a complete roll. During the roll your feet slide sideways so your body turns in place, finishing not parallel but perpendicular to the pool edge. Thus, you do a complete roll and a one-quarter turn. Precision in the roll and the turn are measures of success.

From the start position—floating on your back, parallel to the pool edge, with arms stretched to the sides at shoulder level—sweep your right arm up overhead and your left arm down to your side. Roll onto your right side as you sweep your arms. Continue to roll onto your stomach; sweep your arms back to the outstretched position. Then sweep your left arm overhead and your right arm down to your side as you roll onto your left side. Continue to roll onto your back and sweep your arms back to the starting position. This entire stunt should be done in one continuous, flowing motion.

If you keep your body rigid and make your arms push against the water as they move, you will also turn in place one-quarter turn, finishing perpendicular to the pool edge. As you roll onto your stomach, you may wish to raise your head until your chin is on the water. Keep your entire torso, your legs, your arms, and your wrists rigidly straight throughout the turn; move only from your shoulders. You may, of course, roll in the opposite direction, reverse the movements, and make one-quarter turn also in the opposite direction. Figures 18.1a to e show the marlin turn.

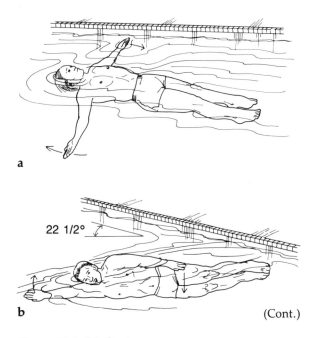

a

b                                    (Cont.)

Figure 18.1  Marlin turn.

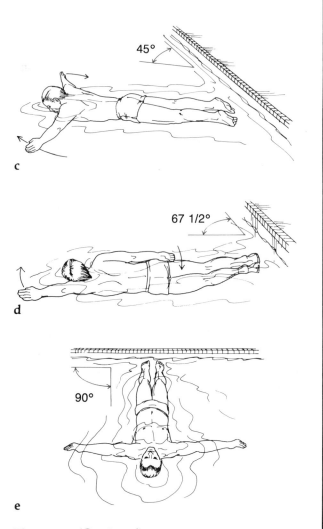

c

d

e

Figure 18.1 (Continued)

## Back Scull Underwater

The back scull underwater is important in the fact that it is a new method of propulsion that you (probably) have not tried. It may surprise you, though. Because of the small expenditure of energy relative to the speed you attain, you may find that you can swim farther underwater this way than by any other method. How will you know until you try it?

For safety, wear defogged goggles and a nose clip or a mask. Start with an underwater push-off from the end of the pool, on your back as from a backstroke turn. As you glide, drop your head back until you can see where you are going. Bring both arms toward your feet until your bent elbows are at your sides, your fingertips pointing directly upward toward the surface. Begin sculling as if you were polishing a tabletop at waist height. The resultant force from this sculling motion will propel you headfirst.

If you begin to rise toward the surface because of buoyancy, bend your wrists a little so your palms face slightly upward toward the surface. The resultant force then will push you headfirst and slightly deeper. Drop your chin occasionally to look upward at the surface to see how deep you are, but for safety look back over your head most of the time. Try to relax your legs and feet as much as you can but keep them streamlined; do not try to kick. If you scull efficiently, you will move rapidly with little fatigue (see Figure 18.2).

Figure 18.2  Back scull underwater.

## Centipede

Did you ever see a centipede swim? This is a multiperson stunt strictly for fun. After a swimming lesson, drill, or workout, lighten up the atmosphere by using a stunt like Centipede as a cooldown.

Get two, three, four, or more people to participate (try to see how many you can get into one centipede). Line them up single file facing the other end of the pool. The first swimmer lies prone and presses his or her feet on the waist of the second swimmer, who puts his or her feet on the waist of the next swimmer, and so on. When every swimmer (except the last) has the feet on the swimmer behind, they all start swimming crawl stroke in rhythm with the lead swimmer. The last swimmer provides the kick for all.

Start with two swimmers and build to as many as possible (see Figure 18.3). Next try a centipede on the back, using a back crawl stroke.

Figure 18.3  A multiperson centipede.

## Play Owl

Face a partner. Both of you take a deep breath and submerge. Move toward each other until you touch noses, and open your eyes as far as you can, like an owl. See if you can do it without laughing. On the other hand, go ahead and laugh. That's what you do when you are having fun.

## Greg Louganis Underwater

Wear a nose clip and goggles. Wear a weight belt with enough weight to make you neutrally buoyant when holding a full breath (with neutral buoyancy, you neither sink nor rise when motionless in the water). Take a breath and do a feetfirst surface dive in 8 feet of water. When your feet touch bottom, immediately push off as though from a diving board and float in slow motion through a perfect one-and-one half somersault with a full twist (or any other dive you wish to emulate or invent). In the weightless environment you can be the perfect diver without the pain of failure. Move over, Greg Louganis!

## Underwater Volleyball

You can create a strange and wonderful creature from a water polo ball. Insert an inflator needle into a water polo ball or a rubber volleyball and squeeze out *all* the air; flatten the ball completely. Now attach a piece of tight-fitting rubber tubing to the needle and put the other end of the tubing into the nozzle of a hose. Turn on the water carefully to fill the ball *completely* with water. Try to work *all* of the air out before withdrawing the inflator needle.

Take the ball into the water and try dribbling it on the bottom like a basketball. See whether you can pass it underwater. It simply will not go straight for more than 2 feet before curving away in some wonderful, unpredictable curves. You can do the same thing with an ordinary balloon filled with water, but it won't last long, and you *must* get all the torn scraps of rubber out of the pool when it breaks.

### Underwater Target Practice

Find a Hula Hoop that floats. Make a small ring of plastic tubing about 8 to 10 inches in diameter; tie it to the Hula Hoop in three places so it becomes a bull's-eye in the center of the Hula Hoop (see Figure 18.4). Collect a few worn-out shuttlecocks from badminton players. Use two colors of waterproof felt-tip pens to mark eight shuttlecocks, four in each color.

Float the hoop target on the surface and swim under it. As you pass under the target, release one or more of the shuttlecocks to float upward to the target. Keep score if you wish.

### WHAT ELSE CAN YOU INVENT?

Ask a synchronized swimmer how to do a waterwheel. Try it. Then see whether you can do it vertically instead of horizontally. Can you maintain a steady lifting motion to hold your legs out of the water up to your knees? How about a frog crawl (a crawl stroke with a frog kick)? Can you do a plank? Try a chain dolphin. How about a tub? Synchronized swimming books are loaded with good stunts.

Have you tried water polo or underwater hockey? Both are sports that are recognized nationwide. Why not take an American Red Cross course in lifeguarding? Become a certified Water Safety Instructor and teach others the joy you have found in aquatics. Join a swim club and be a competitive speed swimmer. If you love the aquatic medium, you will soon be totally immersed in it.

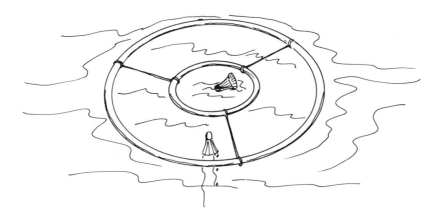

**Figure 18.4**  Target ring from a Hula Hoop.

# Rating Your Total Progress

You have attained many goals in this second-level swimming course. Your skill level has probably risen, but an equally important objective has been the development of an eager, enthusiastic attitude toward the water and to aquatics in general. The following self-rating inventory should lead you to some interesting conclusions. Read the questions thoughtfully and answer them with care.

## ATTITUDINAL CHANGES

Think back to the day this course began. Can you remember your attitude toward the course? Think about your expectations: What did you think the course would do for you, or could do to you? Remember the reasons you decided to enroll for this course rather than for another.

*Your attitude toward water activities in general has changed*

_____ not at all.

_____ a little.

_____ a moderate amount.

_____ a lot.

*Your attitude change has led you toward*

_____ greater fear of water.

_____ dislike of water.

_____ feeling of greater mastery over water.

_____ greater comfort in the water.

_____ joy of being in the water.

*You believe that you truly understand what the text means by the term* watermanship

_____ not at all.

_____ somewhat.

_____ very much.

*As a result of having taken this course, you will*

_____ turn away from water activities.

_____ continue with water activities.

_____ actively seek more water activities.

## PHYSICAL SKILLS

Improvement in physical swimming skills is another objective of the course. How do you rate yourself on the strokes and skills you learned?

|  | Very good | Good | Fair | Poor |
|---|---|---|---|---|
| Crawl stroke | _____ | _____ | _____ | _____ |
| Back crawl stroke | _____ | _____ | _____ | _____ |
| Butterfly stroke | _____ | _____ | _____ | _____ |
| Breaststroke | _____ | _____ | _____ | _____ |
| Sidestroke | _____ | _____ | _____ | _____ |
| Overarm sidestroke | _____ | _____ | _____ | _____ |

|                          | Very good | Good | Fair | Poor |
|--------------------------|-----------|------|------|------|
| Trudgen stroke           | —         | —    | —    | —    |
| Double trudgen stroke    | —         | —    | —    | —    |
| Trudgen crawl stroke     | —         | —    | —    | —    |
| Crawl stroke turns       | —         | —    | —    | —    |
| Back crawl stroke turns  | —         | —    | —    | —    |
| Breaststroke turns       | —         | —    | —    | —    |
| Universal sculling       | —         | —    | —    | —    |
| Surface diving           | —         | —    | —    | —    |
| Underwater swimming      | —         | —    | —    | —    |
| Unconventional strokes   | —         | —    | —    | —    |

## OVERALL PROGRESS

Considering all the attitudinal and physical skill factors you have marked, you would rate your overall progress as

____ unsuccessful.

____ barely successful.

____ successful.

____ very successful.

## ADDITIONAL COMMENTS

Write down any questions that should have been asked but weren't—and answer them, too. Then reflect on the profile that has emerged. What are your strong points in aquatics? Do you want to build upon them? Your weak points? Do you care enough to put more time and effort into strengthening them? Were there things about the course that you would have liked changed, and were these due to the course structure, the instructor, or other factors? What did you like best about this course? How has taking this course benefited you?

# About the Author

David G. Thomas has been a swimming teacher and coach since 1948, when he became a water safety field representative for the American National Red Cross. In 1955 he became swimming coach and director of aquatics at Berea High School, Berea, OH. Eight years later he moved to the State University of New York at Binghamton, where he was director of aquatics and swimming coach until retiring as professor emeritus in 1985.

Thomas gained nationwide prominence in 1972 by producing a textbook, a teaching guide, exams, and visual aids for training swimming pool operators. The *Swimming Pool Operators Handbook* and the other materials were published by the National Swimming Pool Foundation as the basis for their Certified Pool Operators program.

Thomas has published many articles on aquatic subjects and is a contributing author to several books on swimming pool design and operation. He has written extensively since retirement, including the Leisure Press books *Swimming: Steps to Success, Teaching Swimming: Steps to Success, Professional Aquatic Management* (coauthored with Robert Clayton), and *Competitive Swimming Management*. Self-employed as a consultant in aquatics and pool design and operation, Thomas lives with his wife, Virginia, in Anderson, SC, where he enjoys swimming for fitness and boating.